THE MOBBING OF JESUS CHRIST

LISA JOHNSON

Dedication

Facts change when new ideas are accepted as truth. I have provided a different set of facts concerning the life and teachings of Jesus based upon new ideas that have come to light in recent years regarding the effects of bullying and mobbing behavior on the human psyche.

I would like to dedicate this book to the naive ones.
The *nice* ones. The ones who think it will never happen to them because they are *good*.

Other books by Lisa Johnson:

Collectively Wrong

Morality Within The Framework of Reality

Patterns of Peter and Paul

The Evolution of Good and Evil

CONTENTS

Introduction

My previous two books titled, *The Evolution of Good and Evil* and *Patterns of Peter and Paul*, focus on the role of the human ego in creating patterns of thinking that result in what the Bible calls evil actions. The systemic Bully/Bystander/Enabler/Target Model of Thought and Behavior that I describe in *The Evolution of Good and Evil* is a manifestation of these patterns of thinking and it is this model of behavior that underpins all instances of bullying and mobbing, including that of Jesus.

As I document in that book, the concepts of good and evil are not opposites as we have been led to believe by religions that talk about God and Satan as if they are two separate entities of some sort who are constantly in battle with one another. If that were so, then religion would have had this problem of evil licked centuries ago because when an enemy is well defined and easily identified, a strategy can be implemented to counter and defeat it. It is when the enemy quits wearing uniforms and blends into the environment that warfare becomes much more dangerous and ill-defined.

America won the revolutionary war because they knew their environment. The revolutionaries developed a strategy for using the environment in their favor against an enemy that was unable to adjust its methods of warfare to fit the situation. The British soldiers set themselves up like ducks in a shooting gallery as they marched in highly formalized regiments of uniformed soldiers who were easily identified across a forested landscape that provided plenty of cover in which the enemy could hide in plain clothes and pick them off one-by-one.

Some would consider the American revolutionaries to be dirty fighters breaking all the conventional rules of warfare. In British parlors and board rooms, I am certain the American revolutionaries were described as sub-human rodents willing to employ any tactic of the jungle. However, the revolutionaries won the war with their tactics and were therefore able to write their history in a way that views them and their country as morally superior and behaviorally exceptional.

History is always written by the victors, which is why Jesus has such an ambivalent history and legacy. As I will show, he was neither victorious in rising from the dead as Christianity tells us, nor was he a complete fraud and impostor as the Pharisee chief priests defined him. (Matthew 27:62-64) It is my belief that Jesus was a highly evolved and conscious man who made some choices which have allowed both Christianity and Judaism to perceive him in a manner that furthers their religious and doctrinal agendas; but which fails to analyze those choices from a rational standpoint that makes more sense in an age of reason. That is what I try to do with this book. I have attempted to separate the man from the religions and look at some of the facts provided to us in the New Testament, as well as in the scriptures and scrolls that have been labeled as heresy by the Church, but which nonetheless shed more light on the man's history and environment.

Although Christians exalt him as the savior of mankind, the Jews have been much more circumspect about the man and his legacy. From the time the Jewish chief priests branded him an impostor [Matthew 27:62-65] and threatened anyone who acknowledged Jesus as the Messiah with expulsion from the Temple, up until the present day when it is considered a terrible sin for his name to be uttered in certain Jewish homes and children are disowned when they convert to Christianity;[1] Jesus has maintained a checkered legacy that instills both love and hate in the hearts of men and women depending upon where their moral teachings lie. (Matthew 27:63 and John 9:22) It wasn't much different in his own day when many in the community viewed him as exceptional and others took offense at his stepping out of his box as the son of Mary and Joseph. (Matthew 13:54-56)

I think everyone experiences this dichotomy of perception in their own life experiences. We are neither loved by everyone nor are we hated. We are perceived as deserving of love or deserving of hate based upon the eye of the beholder. I know in my own life experience, people have either liked me or disliked me to varying degrees. That is probably the case for most people. I know it was for Jesus. John 7:12-13 says, "There was considerable murmuring about him in the crowds. Some said, "He is a good man [while] others said, "No; on the contrary, he misleads the crowd."

One must always combat perception to arrive at truth. Arriving at truth is a difficult exercise because perception is usually intertwined with one's world view and world views are not so easily abandoned because they serve as a foundation for survival in this physical world where ideologies, philosophies, values and cultures differ so widely.

A very profound example of how intransigent world views can be in the face of facts came to light recently in the most expansive study yet done into the existence of an afterlife. A little over 2,000 people participated in the study. Of the 330 participants who were considered dead, ie., their hearts had stopped beating and their brains had shut down, 140 of them were said to have experienced some sort of awareness during resuscitation; ranging from seeing a bright light to describing everything that happened to them in the operating room while in a state defined as dead. And so, what conclusion did the scientists who conducted the study make to explain this state of awareness occurring after what has been scientifically defined as the point of death? Answer: There may be a small amount of life after death.

Instead of changing their paradigm that life ceases when the brain shuts down in order to consider the possibility that a consciousness exists apart from the physical body it inhabits on this physical plane, these scientists would rather sound foolish and irrational by pushing the bar and saying that life could possibly go on for a little bit of time after the brain shuts down. To me, it sounds a bit like someone saying they are a little bit pregnant. However, no matter how it sounds, these scientists would rather change the facts to fit their paradigm than to let those facts create a new paradigm.

One of the most glaring historical examples of someone who was punished for trying to arrive at truth by combating perception is that of Galileo. During the time he lived, it was the consensus opinion that the sun revolved around the earth, until Copernicus theorized it was the other way around. When Galileo publicly supported Copernicus' theory, he was convicted of heresy and spent the remainder of his life under house arrest. His inquisitors relied upon the following Bible verses to support their case:

> Psalms 93:1: "The LORD reigns, He is clothed with majesty; The LORD has clothed and girded Himself with strength; Indeed, the world is firmly established, it will not be moved."

> Psalms 96:10: "Say among the nations, "The LORD reigns; Indeed, the world is firmly established, it will not be moved; He will judge the peoples with equity."

> Psalms 104:5: "He established the earth upon its foundations, So that it will not totter forever and ever."

> 1 Chronicles 16:30: "Tremble before Him, all the earth; Indeed, the world is firmly established, it will not be moved."

When read literally, these verses do say that the earth does not move. Galileo was a devout Catholic who was also logical. His logical argument that a metaphysical interpretation of these verses was aligned with the scientific model of Copernicus fell on deaf ears; not because it wasn't true (which it was), but rather because it ran counter to the literal interpretation of the verses made by the people in charge. They were not interested in discovering truth as much as they were in silencing Galileo.[1] Ironically, Galileo provided the bridge between science and religion almost 500 years ago, but the hierarchy in power disregarded it because it was not in their personal self-interests to find alignment between the two fields of study. The separation remains in place to this day for the very same reason.

As the example of Galileo illustrates, good and evil/right and wrong do not exist in reality. These concepts exist in how we see, perceive and interpret reality. If powerful individuals within the environmental hierarchy see, perceive and interpret it one way, then their power gives them the environmental tools for silencing any dissenting viewpoints if they so choose. In our evolutionary war between what is perceived as good and what is perceived as evil, evil is winning and will always win until we expose it as an enemy that has written human history in its favor. Knowledge, logic, rationality and truth are the weapons of warfare in this war and the battle cry is Jesus' persistent reminder to his followers and disciples telling them, "Anyone who has ears, ought to hear." (Matthew 11:15, Matthew 13:43, Mark 4:9, Luke 8:8).

1
The Teacher from Galilee

B ecause human perception is at the heart of what the Bible calls good and evil, it was Jesus who pointed us in the right direction when he said our patterns of thought should become the focus of our morality. Jesus was teaching the two-pronged message that salvation of the nation could only come through salvation of the individual. He was up against almost insurmountable odds in getting us to understand that the battle to be fought is within ourselves when we work to align our thoughts with a consciousness of reality and truth, rather than the perception of reality and truth our individual world views provide us.

The Pharisee priests Jesus was constantly doing verbal battle with had a very strong world view based upon the hundreds of laws Moses passed to govern the Israelites who begged him to create them when they were unable to govern themselves with the ten laws of God chiseled in stone. Those ten commandments would have protected them individually and collectively if they were able to break free of the slave mentality they were indoctrinated with in Egypt.[1]

---

[1] I write extensively about the story of Moses and the Israelites in my book, *Collectively Wrong*, and how it really is a story about breaking free from the societal structures that enslave our minds in order to become conscious individuals who protect the community at large by protecting the sanctity of our own individual mind. It is what Jesus taught and it is the message of the entire Bible that has gotten lost in the societal structure of religion.

However, as the Israelites argued to Moses, at least they had food on the table in Egypt.

The Israelites had a survival mentality that allowed them to put up with a lot – even slavery. Their slave masters depended on them keeping a survival mentality so they would choose to remain as slaves and not be captivated by a man like Moses who provided them with a different way to think that would eventually lead to prosperity for them all (the land of milk and honey).

As I will show, Jesus was providing the Jewish people with the same kind of vision that would bring them out from under the thumb of their Pharisaic leadership. The Pharisees loved all the laws passed by Moses because it gave them the levers of control over the Jewish people that kept them in line. Jesus, probably a Pharisee himself as I will also show, tried without success to steer the minds of his Pharisaic colleagues in a different direction by telling them things like, "For out of the heart come evil thoughts, murders, adulteries, fornications, thefts, false witness, slanders. These are the things which defile the man; but to eat with unwashed hands does not defile the man." (Matthew 15:19-20, Mark 7:21-23)

Jesus was prompted to say this to some Pharisees when he and his disciples were chastised for not following the tradition of the elders that required them to wash their hands before eating. Mind you, the Pharisees were men who used their traditions to make a mockery of their own souls. These were men who convinced themselves they were good men because they followed all their traditions. Jesus was, in effect, trying to tell them that they were brainwashed by their mosaic laws, doctrines and traditions to the detriment of their own minds' inherent logic.

The New Testament Gospels of Jesus consistently show the Pharisees to be liars, snobs, thieves, defamers and killers, yet to eat with unwashed hands or do work on the Sabbath, was what was sinful in their eyes. In Matthew 15:6-9, Jesus says to them:

"And by this you invalidated the word of God for the sake of your tradition. You hypocrites, rightly did Isaiah prophesy of you: "This people honors me with their lips, but their heart is far away from me. But in vain do they worship me, teaching as doctrines the precepts of men."" (Matthew 15:6-9)

Through the Pharisees, Jesus is also telling us in this passage that rituals like fasting or attending church every Sunday and outward behaviors like eating with unwashed hands or counting our rosary beads do not determine our character. A person's character materializes through the way that person thinks. What we 'do' will never determine 'who' we are because who we are determines the motive for why we do what we do. Belief systems comprised of doctrines and human precepts that judge people based upon outward appearances (like eating with unwashed hands) allow evil to metastasize throughout an organism because they allow evil to hide behind the veneer of goodness and righteousness. In other words, they allow good and evil to be perceived as good and evil instead of what they really are, and perception is a man-made construct that can too easily be manipulated to fit our individual world views.

We continue to live in a world where men like the Pharisees make a mockery of human thought. We live in a world where politicians are successful in using the name of the God of Creation as justification for their wars of destruction against fellow human beings they have labeled as the enemy. As I will show, it is the same world in which Jesus lived where the High Priest Caiaphas could use the *in the interest of national security* argument to have Jesus eliminated and still feel good about himself. (John 11:48-50)

In the following passages, Jesus tries to relay to the Pharisees that action follows thought. If their thoughts are irrational and corrupted by their strict adherence to the letter of the law, then their actions will be wrong:

Matthew 12:33-35: "Either make the tree good and its fruit good, or make the tree bad and its fruit bad; for the tree is known by its fruit. You brood of vipers, how can you, being evil, speak what is good? For the mouth speaks out of that which fills the heart. The good man brings out of *his* good treasure what is good; and the evil man brings out of *his* evil treasure what is evil.

and

Mark 7:18-23: "Do you not understand that whatever goes into the man from outside cannot defile him, because it does not go into his heart, but into his stomach, and is eliminated?" (*Thus He* declared all foods clean.) And He was saying, "That which proceeds out of the man, that is what defiles the man. For from within, out of the heart of men, proceed the evil thoughts, fornications, thefts, murders, adulteries, deeds of coveting *and* wickedness, *as well as* deceit, sensuality, envy, slander, pride *and* foolishness. All these evil things proceed from within and defile the man."

As these verses make clear, our thinking should be the focus of our morality. Instead, we have placed our focus on outward human behavior to create our morality and judge each person accordingly. When we become dependent on other people to provide us with the doctrines, precepts, beliefs and laws to guide our behaviors, then we turn our individual destinies over to those people. If the truth of our inner being conflicts with their precepts and laws, then we must decide to either quelch it to keep from rocking the boat and suffering the consequences; or follow it and suffer the punishment meted out for acting in conflict with those doctrines and laws. Galileo suffered house arrest for the rest of his life, the dissidents in Nazi Germany were jailed, killed or sent to concentration camps and Jesus was stalked, harassed and ultimately crucified. Many homosexuals stayed closeted and continue to do so to this day because of fear of what coming out will cost them. So many students have given up their individual destinies in their attempts to be perceived as cool in the eyes of their fellow students and so many voices of change in our governments, schools and workplaces have been silenced by the monster disguised as consensus.

Jesus focused on thought patterns because he lived in a world, not unlike our own, where the focus of our morality continues to be based on human precepts rather than universal laws. Universal laws are what the Bible refers to as the laws of God, what secularists refer to as the laws of nature and what humanists refer to as the laws of man. These universal laws have yet to be identified and categorized into a useful format for guiding human thought and behavior, so we continue to rely on religious doctrine and man-made laws to provide the guidance for us.

Living a life consistent with the truth and integrity of one's inner being can be so difficult, particularly in cultures and societies that have passed laws against it. It is understandable that people become fearful of rocking the boat; but when fear of what we may lose by following our consciousness of reality and truth becomes the motivating factor for doing what we do, then we become very prone to doing things we would not otherwise do.

I think Jesus' 40 days in the wilderness, an account of which is found in Matthew 4:1-11 and Luke 4:1-13, is a metaphorical take on Jesus's own personal battle with fear of what he knew would inevitably result from aligning all his thoughts with a consciousness of reality and truth and choosing to teach that truth in an environment of Pharisaic minds who saw the truth as a direct threat to their power and control over the Jewish community. When Jesus came out of the wilderness of a mind doing battle with its own perceptions of what good and evil is, he had a clearly defined purpose for where he wanted to take his life. Freeing himself of the mind clutter he had acquired over a lifetime gave him a supreme sense of confidence and peace, as represented by the devil leaving him and the angels ministering to him in Matthew 4:11.

> "Again, the devil took Him to a very high mountain and showed Him all the kingdoms of the world and their glory; and he said to Him, "All these things I will give You, if You fall down and worship me." Then Jesus said to him, "Go, Satan! For it is written, 'YOU SHALL WORSHIP THE LORD YOUR GOD, AND SERVE HIM ONLY.'" Then the devil left Him; and behold, angels came and *began* to minister to Him.'" (Matthew 4:8-11)

Jesus was not filled with the holy spirit of Christianity in the wilderness. He was a man brought back in touch with himself and what he wanted for his life. Anyone who reads the passages about Jesus's wilderness journey without the fog of religious teachings about spirits and demons can clearly see that Jesus was a man who was at war with himself. He was visibly at some crossroad in his life where he had to make a decision about whether he wanted to pursue a life path that would bring him great power and prestige or whether he wanted to take an alternate path that would not reimburse him financially but would be a path his own mind had decided was right and good for him.

If one is to fully understand Jesus' 40 days in the wilderness. one must abandon the religious view of God as the omnipotent and all-knowing guy in the sky and the devil as his evil counterpart. In my book, *The Evolution of Good and Evil,* I explain how God represents the truth that Adam and Eve abandon in the Garden of Eden. When God allegorically takes a stroll through the Garden and discovers that the Man and Woman he put there are wearing fig leaves, God knows the reason why. Every one of his 'why' questions that follow are meant to get the Man and Woman to see the 'why' of what they did. Instead of examining themselves to determine why they ate from the tree of knowledge of good and evil when they were told not to (their motive), they choose to lie and blame one another and the snake rather than face up to the truth of themselves. (Genesis 3:8-13)

'Why' questions are never welcomed in toxic, corrupt environments like the one Eve created in the Garden or the one in which Jesus found himself. The title of a book by Rachel Roth, a holocaust survivor writing about her own experience, is *"Here There Is No Why."* The title is the answer that Dr. Joseph Mengele gave to her and to all the other Jews targeted by the Nazi regime who asked him 'why'. Why questions are questions corrupt people will never ask or answer because they requires them to look within themselves to determine the motive for why they do what they do. In the case of Mengele and the other members of the Nazi SS, it was so much easier to just follow the orders of their superiors and do what they were told. To a greater or lesser extent, they all knew at some level of their consciousness that if they were to do the self-analysis and arrive at the conclusion that what they were doing was wrong and refused to follow those orders (human precepts set out by their leader), then they would end up in the same boat as their Jewish and dissident targets. You can see how asking 'why' posed a problem for Mengele and the Nazi regime he served. If he attempted to honestly answer the question, it would prove his culpability, guilt and greed in the theft, torture and murder of millions of his fellow human beings.

It is no accident that many progressive companies rely on the Six Sigma 5-whys of process improvement to improve the way they do business. Asking why questions help us drill down to the root cause of any problem so we can fix it. Alternatively, corrupt environments that rely on the destruction of truth in favor of perception avoid asking why questions at all costs.

If the allegory of Adam and Eve tells us anything, it is that the God of creation is the God of reality and truth. As science is proving almost daily, God uses universal laws based in logic and mathematics to create this multiverse we inhabit. Logic and mathematics tell us that $a+a+a = 3a$. It can never equal $3b$ or $1a$. It is a formula that is intransient in its truth. Adam and Eve know the truth when they know that they are not to eat from the tree of knowledge of good and evil. It is only when the snake undermines the truth by convincing Eve to eat the fruit with a false argument she never bothers to question, that she loses sight of the truth in favor of creating her own truth that better suits her individual self-interests:

> "Now the serpent was more crafty than any beast of the field which the LORD God had made. And he said to the woman, "Indeed, has God said, 'You shall not eat from any tree of the garden'?" The woman said to the serpent, "From the fruit of the trees of the garden we may eat; but from the fruit of the tree which is in the middle of the garden, God has said, 'You shall not eat from it or touch it, or you will die.'" The serpent said to the woman, "You surely will not die! For God knows that in the day you eat from it your eyes will be opened, and you will be like God, knowing good and evil." When the woman saw that the tree was good for food, and that it was a delight to the eyes, and that the tree was desirable to make *one* wise, she took from its fruit and ate; and she gave also to her husband with her, and he ate." (Genesis 3:1-6)

I write in some length in my book, *The Evolution of Good and Evil*, that the snake that confronts Eve in the Garden and Jesus in the wilderness represents the human ego. The fact that Jesus remained true to his internal source code after going head-to-head with his own ego is the symbolism of the Holy Spirit descending upon him like a dove after his baptism by John the Baptist. (Luke 3:22) His 40 days in the wilderness was his own personal testing ground to ensure he could resist the pressures he knew he would encounter so that he could always practice what he was preaching.

Unlike Jesus, the woman, Eve, does not resist her ego's arguments to eat the fruit. When she instead accepts those arguments as true, she goes from knowing the fruit of the tree is forbidden to perceiving it as pleasing to the eye and desirable to eat and she does it by making her consciousness of truth (God) the bad guy. Truth always becomes the bad guy when we lie to ourselves. That is what makes the truth so hard for most people to hear. They have already convinced themselves of the righteousness of the lies they have told themselves. Adam is merely a bystander who becomes Eve's enabler when she convinces him to take a bite out of the fruit as well; probably using the same false arguments on him as the snake uses on her.

Jesus was discovering the inner truth of his being in his wilderness journey that Eve abandons in the Garden and that the Pharisees replaced with human precepts and laws. He was ridding his mind of the same false assumptions, lies and self-interested motives that Eve was unable to overcome. As I will prove in this book, Jesus went into his wilderness journey as an expert in the law like his Pharisee colleagues and came out committed to teaching what he knew to be true about the Jewish scriptures.

Once we begin to embrace the concept of God and Satan/good and evil as the creative consciousness of truth and reality and alternatively, the destructive consciousness of falsehood and perception, then the wilderness journey becomes a journey we all must take when our internal assumptions and beliefs are making it difficult for us to be true to ourselves and to the calling of our souls. By rejecting the same false arguments offered to Eve, Jesus remained true to the desires of his inner being. It caused him to make a choice he knew would create conflict with his family, colleagues and friends, but which made him totally at peace with himself.

John the Baptist, a mentor and friend of Jesus, also did battle with the Pharisees. He tells them in Matthew 3:7-12, "You brood of vipers! Who warned you to flee from the coming wrath? Produce good fruit as evidence of your repentance. ... I am baptizing you with water, for repentance, but the one who is coming after me is mightier than I. He will baptize you with the holy Spirit and fire." Of course, he is speaking of Jesus.

Unlike John the Baptist, Jesus never baptized anyone in water, just as he didn't command his disciples to fast. (John 4:1-2 and Matthew 2:18-22) He had no interest in rituals and human traditions because rituals and human traditions become rather pointless when looked at through a lens of truth. Why perform them? What is the point? What are people trying to prove when they give up chocolate for Lent or submerge themselves in a vat of water? Jesus said it a whole lot better when he asked the Pharisees, "Why do you break the commandment of God for the sake of your tradition? ...You have nullified the word of God for the sake of your tradition. Hypocrites, well did Isaiah prophesy about when he said: 'This people honors me with their lips, but their hearts are far from me; in vain do they worship me, teaching as doctrines human precepts." (Matthew 15:3-9)

Jesus was as real as they come. His teachings, which I detail throughout this book, all deal with the inherent conflicts that arise between a mind that wants to live in reality and truth and a mind that feels it must conform to alternate assumptions and beliefs in order to survive mentally, emotionally, physically and financially within the cultural norms and structures of any given man-made society. His teachings are the baptismal holy Spirit and fire for all human beings who want to break free of all the mind clutter which blocks us from discovering our true selves and purpose.

Just like John the Baptist, one of Jesus' central tenets was that of repentance. Matthew 4:17 says, "From that time on [after learning of the arrest of John the Baptist], Jesus began to preach and say, "Repent, for the kingdom of heaven is at hand." (See Matthew 4:17).

There are three Greek words used in the New Testament to denote repentance: the verb metamelomai, and the verb metanoeo when used with the noun metanoia.[2] All three words connote a change of one's mind and purpose and life. Changing one's mind, purpose and life while living in a society like that of the people to which Jesus was preaching can prove to be a very dangerous proposition. They were not only under the thumb of their Pharisee scribes; they were also under the totalitarian rule of Caesar.

When repentance became a central tenet of Jesus' teachings, he became a revolutionary at the level of one. That is the most dangerous kind there is for hierarchical power structures who know how to control the group with all their laws and regulations, but who fear a dissident voice like the plague for fear it will awaken the holy spirit of purpose and life within us all. Martin Luther King was one of those voices, along with so many other whistle blowers and truth tellers who have been fired from their jobs, denied tenure, isolated, marginalized, tortured, jailed and killed just for speaking out about what they viewed as reality and truth.

Jesus was a rabbi doing battle with the world view of his own Jewish community and it is what made him such a divisive figure both then and now. He was a seeker of truth in a world where truth, more often than not, shines the light on the fallacies of our world views. Jesus began stepping on some very powerful toes when he used the Pharisees as examples of who not to be. Real life examples always drive a message home better than theoretical musings and the Pharisees provided such great material for showing his audience how not to think and behave. He went straight for the jugular in the verses in Matthew 23 where he calls them fools, hypocrites and vipers. If there is anything a person with a strong world view hates more than to be proven wrong, it is for other people to witness it.

Matthew 23:1-36: "Then Jesus spoke to the crowds and to His disciples, saying: "The scribes and the Pharisees have seated themselves in the chair of Moses; therefore all that they tell you, do and observe, but do not do according to their deeds; for they say *things* and do not do *them*. They tie up heavy burdens and lay them on men's shoulders, but they themselves are unwilling to move them with *so much as* a finger. But they do all their deeds to be noticed by men; for they broaden their phylacteries and lengthen the tassels *of their garments*. They love the place of honor at banquets and the chief seats in the synagogues, and respectful greetings in the market places, and being called Rabbi by men, ... "But woe to you, scribes and Pharisees, hypocrites, because you shut off the kingdom of heaven from people; for you do not enter in yourselves, nor do you allow those who are entering to go in. Woe to you, scribes and Pharisees, hypocrites, because you devour widows' houses, and for a pretense you make long prayers; therefore you will receive greater condemnation.]"Woe to you, scribes and Pharisees, hypocrites, because you travel around on sea and land to make one proselyte; and when he becomes one, you make him twice as much a son of hell as yourselves. "Woe to you, blind guides, who say, 'Whoever swears by the temple, *that* is nothing; but whoever swears by the gold of the temple is obligated.' You fools and blind men! Which is more important, the gold or the temple that sanctified the gold? ... "Woe to you, scribes and Pharisees, hypocrites! For you tithe mint and dill and cummin, and have neglected the weightier provisions of the law: justice and mercy and faithfulness; but these are the things you should have done without neglecting the others. You blind guides, who strain out a gnat and swallow a camel! "Woe to you, scribes and Pharisees, hypocrites! For you clean the outside of the cup and of the dish, but inside they are full of robbery and self-indulgence. You blind Pharisee, first clean the inside of the cup and of the dish, so that the outside of it may become clean also. "Woe to you, scribes and Pharisees, hypocrites! For you are like whitewashed tombs which on the outside appear beautiful, but inside they are full of dead men's bones and all uncleanness. So you, too, outwardly appear righteous to men, but inwardly you are full of hypocrisy and lawlessness. "Woe to you, scribes and Pharisees, hypocrites! For you build the tombs of the prophets and adorn the monuments of the righteous, and say, 'If we had been *living* in the days of our fathers, we would not have been partners with them in *shedding* the blood of the prophets.' So you testify against yourselves, that you are sons of those who murdered the prophets. Fill up, then, the measure *of the guilt* of your fathers. You serpents, you brood of vipers, how will you escape the sentence of hell?"

I have heard the expression, "Do as I say, not as I do," all my life and never had any idea it originated with Jesus. In his condemnation of the religious hierarchy of his day in the above passage, Jesus is telling the crowd to whom he is speaking that the Pharisees hide all their corruption and hypocrisy behind the veneer of righteousness. He compares them to whitewashed tombs which appear beautiful on the outside, but inside are full of dead men's bones and all uncleanness. In other words, what the Pharisees were saying and what they were doing were two completely different things. They cultivated an image for the outside world to see, but personally conducted their lives as they pleased. They stole money from poor widows while at the same time praying for their souls; they preached a legalistic doctrine that they themselves refused to follow; they offered their tithes to the temple but neglected their own responsibility as human beings to be just and merciful towards those less fortunate and they condemned their ancestors for killing prophets when, as I will show in the rest of this book, they themselves were plotting to kill Jesus at the time Jesus was saying all this.

The Pharisees and Sadducees were the elite of their day who think it is criminal for the family living paycheck-to-paycheck not to pay their share of taxes but who hide their own money in tax havens created for the wealthy. They were the company executives who get their kids' college education paid for, but who see nothing wrong in making their secretaries and clerks muddle by on minimum wage with no hope of ever being able to send their children to college. They were the politicians of their day who pass health care laws that dictate terms and coverage for their constituents but who exempt themselves from the law so that they can choose their own coverage. They were all the religious preachers and teachers who preach a prosperity message to their followers so that they can feel better about themselves for having conformed their own minds to materialism and greed. Worst of all, they were the spiritual gurus of their day who tell us that love is the answer when they know that all the love in the world will not affect people like the Pharisees who have conformed their minds to corrupted assumptions and beliefs needed to ascend the man-made ladders of success. As we climb these ladders to grab the carrots of materialism at each step, we conform our way of thinking to what is required for material success. And that conformance often requires us to adjust our motive for behavior to what our bosses require of us, what the bottom-line dictates and what the shareholders demand.

The Pharisees were drowning in perks that their positions provided but they were ill-gotten perks obtained off the backs of people who were struggling to keep their heads above water from one day to the next. Jesus knew the Pharisee vipers loved money above all else. It was them he was speaking to in Luke 16:10-13 when he said, "The person who is trustworthy in very small matters is also trustworthy in great ones; and the person who is dishonest in very small matters is also dishonest in great ones. If therefore, you are not trustworthy with dishonest wealth, who will trust you with true wealth. ...No servant can serve two masters. He will either hate one and love the other, or be devoted to one and despise the other. You cannot serve God and mammon."

The very next verse says, "The Pharisees, who loved money, heard all these things and sneered at him." The Merriam-Webster online dictionary defines a sneer as, "a contemptuous or mocking smile, remark, or tone." They clearly hated Jesus, and their sneers said it all. They were so contemptuous of this nobody in their eyes telling them the truth. But not to worry. They were in control of the situation. They knew this messenger would soon be killed along with his message. These cowardly, sneering, hateful Pharisee vipers perched at the top of their Pharisaic hierarchy sneered at him all the way to the cross they put him on. It wasn't God who put him there. It is complete heresy to be told that God sent Jesus to die on the cross. The God of creation creates. It doesn't destroy. It is the corrupt, human mind that chooses destruction as a means of righting wrongs. It is time to separate the chaff from the wheat and look at Jesus and his fate with realistic eyes.

I do not treat Jesus' story as a religious story in this book. I treat it as the very real story of a man who was working within a corrupt religious environment where the politics of power took priority over the truth. By any religious standard, Jesus should have been defended and protected. Instead, the religious leaders of his day made people perceive him as a criminal deserving of one of the most horrific methods of execution ever devised by mankind; just so they could get their win and protect their turf. They turned the tables on Jesus and to do so, they had to turn over truth itself. They used the Bully-Bystander-Enabler-Target Model of Thought and Behavior to make their actions of killing a righteous man appear reasonable, logical and truthful among the general public. Although their actions were none of those things, they got away with the killing by using their power to create an alternate paradigm.

2

Mobbing Defined

The dysfunctional paradigm between truth and what is perceived as truth is what makes bullying and mobbing behavior such a thorny problem in our society. Behaviors labeled as bullying and mobbing are motivated by human perception and human perception can too easily be shaped by those with the power to shape it. Jesus happened to be in a corrupt religious environment where the politics of power took priority over the truth. He was essentially a rabbi who went rogue. Once he decided it was his purpose to teach the true meaning of the scriptures, instead of the legalistic interpretation the Pharisaic power structure preferred, he was cast as the trouble maker who was stirring up people wherever he went:

> "Then the whole body of them got up and brought Him before Pilate. And they began to accuse Him, saying, "We found this man misleading our nation and forbidding to pay taxes to Caesar, and saying that He Himself is Christ, a King." So Pilate asked Him, saying, "Are You the King of the Jews?" And He answered him and said, "*It is as* you say." Then Pilate said to the chief priests and the crowds, "I find no guilt in this man." But they kept on insisting, saying, "<u>He stirs up the people, teaching all over Judea, starting from Galilee even as far as this place.</u>" (Luke 23:1-5)

Jesus - the man who was drawing great crowds from Galilee,

the Decapolis, Jerusalem, Judea and beyond the Jordan; (Matthew 4:25, Luke 6:17-19) the man who was astonishing those very same crowds with his teachings; (Matthew 7:28-29) the man who gave great crowds of people the faith that they could heal themselves – mind, body and soul; (Matthew 9:8, 22) the man who had to escape in a boat for fear that the crowds he was attracting would crush him; (Mark 3:9) the man who entered Jerusalem for his final Passover to a crowd laying their cloaks and tree branches on the road as he passed, crying out "Hosanna to the Son of David; blessed is he who comes in the name of the Lord; hosanna in the highest;" (Matthew 21:6-9, Mark 11:8-10) – this was the man who was labeled a troublemaker and accused of stirring up crowds by his Pharisee colleagues and leaders.

In cases of workplace mobbing, or of any mobbing for that matter, it is important that the competent, targeted individual who is good at his job be perceived as the troublemaker who is causing problems for everyone. The tables of reality and truth must be turned over to make way for the lie of perception. In an article titled, *Mediocrity and the 'No Change' Principle: A Recipe for Mobbing*, Dr. Jocelynne A. Scutt describes how this process works of turning innocent targeted individuals into troublemakers deserving of the abuse the mob is heaping upon them. She explains that mobbing is characterized by a role reversal whereby the innocent is made to look guilty and the guilty get off scot-free because they are perceived as the saviors of the situation:

> "Mobbing is characterized by reversing the roles of the mobbed and the mobber, the bully and the bullied. The prime cry of the mobber is that s/he is being 'bullied' by the change agent. This is designed to undermine the change agent's authority and standing, because it tears at the heart of everything the change agent stands for."[3]

The perpetrators of a mobbing purposely go after their

target's core consciousness so that the targeted individual will feel a sense of worthlessness about themselves. The behavioral manifestations of that sense of worthlessness like anger, fear, paranoia, anxiety and depression make everyone else think the target is the cause of the problems as well and not the power abuser or abusers who initiated the conflict. Since people want to side with the winner, they join in the campaign of degradation and destruction and soon an army of enablers and bystanders are recruited to join the abusive campaign of individual destruction.

If ever there was a change agent, it was Jesus. As I discuss later in the book, this role reversal strategy was employed by the High Priest Caiaphas in his campaign to vilify Jesus and get him executed. Although Christianity has created a perception of Jesus as the manifestation of God on earth, it was not always that way. When his life is viewed through the lens of reality and truth, based upon what we know of it from the Bible's New Testament and the more recently discovered Nag Hammadi library of gnostic gospels, it becomes clear that the High Priest Caiaphas was successful in his campaign to turn Jesus into the bad guy who was a threat to national security. (See John 11:45-53) Caiaphas blatantly and manipulatively used the power of his position to give all the minions below him in the hierarchy the justification they needed to join him in his campaign of ridicule, maliciousness and hate. By the time his campaign was over, Jesus became a man who was perceived as deserving of the death penalty.

It was Caiaphas and others like him who provided the playbook for another of history's master manipulators of truth - Adolf Hitler. Hitler used the same strategy of turning truth on its ear by creating the perception that the Jews were the cause of all of Germany's problems. Once the perception took hold among the general population, it became much easier to target and isolate them. Below is an excerpt from one of many speeches Hitler gave where he painted the Jews as the cause of all of Germany's problems and misery after WWI:

> "I beg you, and particularly those of you who carry the cross throughout the land, to become somewhat more serious when I speak of the enemy of the German people, namely, the Jew. Not out of irresponsibility or for fun do I fight against the Jewish enemy, but because I bear within me the knowledge <u>that the whole misfortune was brought to Germany by the Jews alone</u>. ... You must realise that the Jew wants our people to perish. That is why you must join us and leave those who have brought you nothing but war and inflation and discord. For thousands of years the Jew has been destroying the nations. Let us make a new beginning so that we can annihilate the Jews."[4]

Like Caiaphas, Hitler was a power abuser. Unlike Caiaphas, he was a power abuser with an anti-Semitic world view. However, as Caiaphas and Hitler both show, a mobbing can be instigated against one individual or millions of individuals. The commonality between the two is the use of strategies for manipulating truth to create the perception you want to create to achieve your goal.

Both men were positioned at the top of their respective hierarchies and that position of power gave them access to the means for conforming the minds of the populations they controlled to their way of thinking. Caiaphas rose to his position through family connections and Hitler rose to his position because he was saying all the right things to a tired, poor, hungry and desperate population that was thoroughly worn out from the draconian measures imposed upon them by the Treaty of Versailles.

Powerful connections and false promises are not uncommon avenues for mediocre people to use to climb the ladder of success when they lack other means like intelligence, skills and experience. In fact, it makes these kinds of leaders (if you can call them that) very desperate to retain the status quo for fear that change will result in situations that they are ill-equipped to handle.

Jesus was operating in a very similar environment to that of the German population after World War I. He was teaching a population that was getting it from both ends. They were angry at the taxation and draconian measures of the Roman Empire, and they were also tired of getting fleeced by their Jewish leadership. Jesus was a breath of fresh air who was teaching them how not to feel hopeless and helpless in the controlled and dehumanizing society in which they were forced to survive.

Jesus was clearly the kind of change agent that Dr. Scutt says needs to be undermined. Mobbing is a very effective tool for undermining and ultimately eliminating change agents and other people deemed as troublemakers threatening the status quo. In their book, *Mobbing: Emotional Abuse in the American Workplace*, the authors describe mobbing as a malicious attempt to force a person from the workplace by using unjustified accusations, humiliation, innuendo and rumors which escalate to abusive and terrorizing behavior equivalent to an emotional assault against the target of their actions.[5]

Not infrequently, mobbing activities are directed at whistle blowers. Brian Martin, in Whistle blowing and Nonviolence (Peace and Change, Vol. 24, No. 3, January 1999) describes attacks on whistle blowers this way:

"Whistle blowing, in casual usage, means speaking out from within an organization to expose a social problem or, more generally, dissenting from dominant views or practices... The most common experience of whistle blowers is that they are attacked. Instead of their messages being evaluated, the full power of the organization is turned against the whistle blower. This is commonly called the shoot-the-messenger syndrome ... The means of suppression are impressive, nonetheless. They include ostracism by colleagues, petty harassment (including snide remarks, assignment to trivial tasks and invoking of regulations not normally enforced), spreading of rumors, formal reprimands, transfer to positions with no work (or too much work), demotion, referral to psychiatrists, dismissal, and blacklisting."

I will not go into detail in this book, but there are verses in the Old Testament that match almost verbatim what Jesus says about repentance; judgment; forgiveness; loving God with all your heart, mind and soul; and treating others as you would like to be treated. That knowledge was available to the Pharisees, but kept hidden from the population they controlled with their insistence that all the mosaic laws, in which they were experts, be followed. Jesus was giving the people an alternate paradigm and changing their focus from one of enslavement under the law to one of self-governance.

Jesus counter-intuitively teaches us that if we were to focus on our true existence as energetic (spiritual) beings, rather than as purely physical beings and begin caring first for the quality of our thinking, rather than the conformance of our thinking, we would not only survive – we would thrive because we would be creating a foundation of truth for ourselves and our lives.

As proven by the crowds Jesus was attracting, the people were ready to change their focus. However, their leadership could have none of that. They had to deal with the whistleblower Jesus before their power dissolved under the knowledge Jesus was providing. In their attempt to permanently silence Jesus, they used a shoot-the-messenger process that mobbing/bullying tactics provide.

The Phases of a Mobbing

Mobbing has been found to follow a very stereotypical course from case to case. Heinz Leymann, a doctor at the University of Stockholm and National Institute of Occupational Health in Stockholm, Sweden, studied the mobbing phenomenon in the workplace and referred to it as 'psychic terror."[6] According to Leymann, workplace mobbing involves hostile and unethical communications directed in a systematic way against a targeted individual by a group of individuals in the workplace. These hostile actions, which take place almost every day over a period of time, have five distinct phases as follows:

Phase I: The original critical incident

Phase II: The mobbing and stigmatizing phase

Phase III: The personnel management phase when management becomes involved

Phase IV: The phase in which the targeted employee is incorrectly perceived and diagnosed as being crazy

Phase V: The final phase in which the targeted employee is expelled from the workplace

Losing one's job in such a manner is often accompanied by the corresponding loss of one's career, marriage, health, and livelihood. "From a study of circumstances surrounding suicides in Sweden, Leymann estimated that about twelve percent of people who take their own lives have recently been mobbed at work"[7]

One of the mobbing cases Leymann studied was that of a man he called Leif; a skilled and highly competent Danish factory worker employed in a Norwegian factory. Leif had been successful at every position he held before he became an unemployable outcast with psychological problems after being victimized by a mob of co-workers in this Norwegian factory. They began their hostile campaign against him by making fun of his accent. When they saw that his irritation and resentment over their treatment was irritating him, they stepped up their malicious activity by playing jokes on him. One of their jokes was to send him to repair machines that did not need repair. Since his colleagues didn't know his appearances were the result of jokes being played on him, his reputation deteriorated, and he became known as "The Mad Dane." As his network broke down, more and more of his workmates joined in the mobbing campaign until jokes and taunts followed him wherever he went.

Leif became very angry and his aggression naturally drew the attention of management, who came to perceive him as a problematic employee. When he was admonished for poor performance, he became angrier and more anxious and developed psychosomatic problems which resulted in his taking of sick leave. Because of this, he was assigned to less skilled work without anyone talking to him about what was happening. The feelings of injustice and hopelessness management's actions engendered in him caused his psychological condition to worsen and his sick leaves to lengthen. Eventually, he lost his job and became unemployable in an occupation in which he previously excelled.

According to Kenneth Westhues, a professor of sociology at the University of Waterloo, Ontario, Canada, bullies are very good at convincing coworkers and managers that the targeted individual deserves the abuse to which they are subjected. As the attacks continue day in and day out the target begins to be worn down and eventually will make a mistake. Perhaps they will have an emotional outburst and lash back at the bully. Such incidents are stereotypical in mobbing cases according to Westhues and are used to turn the tables on the targeted individual. It allows the instigator of the bullying and mobbing behavior to claim that the targeted individual is the real troublemaker. It also provides incentive for management, who has failed to take any action up to that point, to punish the wrong party.[8]

Mobbing can be ongoing for years. It can cause health problems and can even cause the targets of it to become violent or have emotional breakdowns. Mobbing is hard to prove, and changing jobs might stop the mobbing, but it may not. Mobbing can cause you to be blacklisted from your field of employment.[9]

As I will spend the rest of this book showing, it was not God who sent Jesus to the cross. It was a malicious attempt by the Pharisee chief priest, Caiaphas and his minions to force a good and righteous man from the workplace through unjustified accusations, humiliation, innuendo and false rumors. Jesus was a victim of mobbing behavior that followed all five phases identified by Leymann. The decisions it caused him to make blurred the lines of truth he cherished so much and changed his life and legacy in ways he never could have foreseen.

3
Phase I: The Original Critical Incident
A Pharisee Gets Triggered

In the initial phase of a mobbing, there is a trigger event or situation that serves to create a conflict between the targeted person and another individual or group of individuals. Leymann identifies this event as the critical incident that serves as a triggering event to a conflict which eventually morphs into a mobbing type of situation.

This first phase of a mobbing is usually very short and transitions into phase 2 very quickly when other work colleagues and members of management get involved. Although not much is known about critical incidents, I would surmise the reason for that lack of knowledge is because any slight or perceived slight can become a trigger for someone who is easily triggered. It could be insecurity over a colleague's competence or even the way someone was spoken to in front of other people. In the case study Leymann used of the factory worker named Leif, the critical incident was someone's envy over Leif's wages.

While some researchers on the subject believe that targets of bullying and mobbing display universal qualities of integrity, a sense of fair play, honesty, trustworthiness, intelligence and creativity; other studies indicate that mobbing behaviors are a symptomatic of a destructive and toxic workplace culture where anyone can potentially become a target.[10] I do not believe the two views are mutually exclusive. In toxic work environments, toxic patterns of thought and behavior are considered normal operating procedure, and anyone can become a target whether they exhibit exceptional qualities or not.

In cases where insecure, character-deficient leaders are put in charge, then it makes sense that people with integrity, a sense of fair play, honesty and trustworthiness would become targets because it is those very qualities that highlight the inadequacies of character-deficient colleagues and bosses who have climbed the ladder of success by having the right pedigree or connections and by getting along with the right people, rather than by having the right experience and skills.

Although there is no way of knowing for certain, the critical incident that triggered the mobbing against Jesus could very likely have arisen over someone's envy of Jesus' popularity and superior intellect. Mark 6:1-3 quotes someone as saying of Jesus, "Who does this man think he is? Isn't he the son of Mary and Joseph the carpenter?" Whoever said this, clearly thought that Jesus was acting uppity and not staying in his lane.

However, there is also no doubt that Jesus was in a toxic work environment where the Pharisees and Sadducees were exempting themselves from the laws and rules they were burdening the rest of the community with, for purposes of retaining their power and control over that community. Jesus had all the qualities that highlighted the deficiencies of his Pharisee colleagues. Jesus was not just a good man. He was a great intellectual and teacher who could not only quote scripture but also analyze it logically.

In fact, Jesus' logic left the Pharisees speechless on several occasions. An example of one such encounter is found in Matthew 22:41-44, where Jesus asks a group of Pharisees the following question: "What is your opinion about the Messiah? Whose son is he?" When they reply in accordance with their doctrine that the Messiah is the son of King David, Jesus asks them how that can be given that David himself refers to him as 'Lord' in Psalm 110:1, which reads, "The LORD says to my Lord: Sit at My right hand until I make Your enemies a footstool for your feet."

Not a one of the Pharisees, all experts in the scriptures and law, were able to answer Jesus' question and verse 45 says that from that day on, no one dared to ask him any questions. Logic will always silence people and leave them speechless when they are holding tight to world views, beliefs and doctrine that have no logical foundation.

As counter intuitive as it sounds, the people most vulnerable to becoming targets of a mobbing are average and high achieving workers whose own good work has somehow made a well-connected co-worker or manager feel threatened or shamed.[11] I think this may have been the case with Jesus because he was putting the Pharisees to shame everywhere he went. The verses found in Luke 13:14-17 specifically say that Jesus' logic, empathy and talents were serving to humiliate the Pharisees in front of the crowds who always surrounded Jesus. In the passage below, Jesus has just cured a woman on the Sabbath and the synagogue official who witnesses it uses the law to justify his false indignation:

> "But the synagogue official, indignant because Jesus had healed on the Sabbath, *began* saying to the crowd in response, "There are six days in which work should be done; so come during them and get healed, and not on the Sabbath day." But the Lord answered him and said, "You hypocrites, does not each of you on the Sabbath untie his ox or his donkey from the stall and lead him away to water *him*? And this woman, a daughter of Abraham as she is, whom Satan has bound for eighteen long years, should she not have been released from this bond on the Sabbath day?" As He said this, all His opponents were being humiliated; and the entire crowd was rejoicing over all the glorious things being done by Him."

Perhaps there is nothing worse for an insecure person in a position of power than to be put to shame in front of other people by someone perceived to be at the bottom of the hierarchy. Jesus was not only putting the Pharisees to shame in private, as evidenced by his interaction regarding King David, but he was also humiliating them in public.

It could have been just one influential person within the group of Pharisees who initiated the campaign of personal destruction against Jesus. Luke 11:37-53 indicates this may be the case. In this passage, Jesus has been invited to dinner by a Pharisee who proceeds to question him about why he is not observing the prescribed washing before the meal. Jesus responds to this Pharisee by telling him:

> "Woe to you Pharisees! For you pay tithe of mint and rue and every *kind of* garden herb, and *yet* disregard justice and the love of God; but these are the things you should have done without neglecting the others. Woe to you Pharisees! For you love the chief seats in the synagogues and the respectful greetings in the market places. Woe to you! For you are like concealed tombs, and the people who walk over *them* are unaware *of it.*" One of the lawyers said to Him in reply, "Teacher, when You say this, You insult us too." (Luke 11:42-45)

The passage above is found in Luke and the wording indicates it is probably the same incident found in Matthew 23 that I quoted earlier where Jesus lambastes the Pharisees calling them snakes, vipers, hypocrites and whitewashed tombs. The verses in Luke end by saying, "When He left there, the scribes and the Pharisees began to be very hostile and to question Him closely on many subjects, plotting against Him to catch Him in something He might say." (Luke 11:53-54)

The truth hurts, particularly when it is given in such a forceful and blunt manner. The Pharisees were not only insulted by what Jesus said, they were infuriated with him and their egos would not allow him to get away with it. Although the hostility may have begun at a dinner with a single Pharisee, it eventually ended with the involvement of the chief priests and the entire Jewish Council out to destroy him.

Prof. Westhues describes how this process works in his article, *At the Mercy of the Mob: A Summary of Research on Workplace Mobbing*. What begins as a grudge initiated by an influential person within a group soon becomes a collective campaign by co-workers to exclude, punish, and humiliate the targeted person. The campaign of personal destruction spreads from one person to the next "like a virus" until eventually, the target of the campaign "comes to be viewed as absolutely abhorrent, with no redeeming qualities, outside the circle of acceptance and respectability, deserving only of contempt. As the campaign proceeds, a steadily larger range of hostile ploys and communications comes to be seen as legitimate.[12]

This certainly appears to be what happened to Jesus. His Pharisee colleagues, with whom he studied the law and some of whom he knew from childhood, spat in his face, blindfolded him and then hit and slapped him after sentencing him to die. (Matthew 26:67, Mark 14:65) But not before they unceasingly hounded him throughout his entire teaching ministry besmirching his character, telling lies about him and trying to trick him into saying something for which they could arrest him. Like the mediocre, envious and uncreative brood of vipers they were; they followed like clockwork the five phases of mobbing that have been identified by Leymann in their campaign to destroy the man they knew was telling the truth. However, it was a truth they could not afford to be heard.

Let's make no mistake about it. Jesus was assassinated using patterns of behavior that are increasingly becoming the status quo in all areas of our society, particularly government and commerce. If the strategies used against him by the power structure of his day had been identified, isolated and communicated to the general public as the evil they are, then our world would be a very different place from what it is today. However, instead of eradicating the patterns of thought and behavior used by the Pharisees to persecute Jesus, the church became one of the most prolific users of these patterns as a means of silencing within its ranks any dissent from the stated doctrine.

Many of the texts excluded from the official Bible that serve as the foundation for church doctrine shed much more light on Jesus' background and history. It appears from these texts that he was not a poor carpenter's son. He was a very educated scholar who was schooled in the law. All his years of schooling are referred to by the church as the 'lost years' of Jesus. They are not so lost if one makes the effort to study some of the texts that have been declared as heresy by the church. The Gospels of Jesus contained in the New Testament Gospels of Matthew, Mark, Luke and John cover three years of Jesus' life. There are thirty years we know nothing about except for the fact that Jesus was debating with teachers of the law in the temple at twelve years of age and all who heard him were astonished at his understanding and answers. [See Luke 2:46-52]

We get a little more detail about this temple encounter in The First Gospel of the Infancy of Jesus Christ where the following account is given:

> "Then a certain principal Rabbi asked him, Hast thou read books? Jesus answered, he had read both books, and the things which were contained in books. And he explained to them the books of the law, and precepts, and statutes: and the mysteries which are contained in the books of the prophets; things which the mind of no creature could reach. Then said that Rabbi, I never yet

have seen or heard of such knowledge! What do you think that boy will be? When a certain astronomer, who was present, asked the Lord Jesus, whether he had studied astronomy? The Lord Jesus replied and told him the number of the spheres and heavenly bodies, as also their triangular, square, and sextile aspect; their progressive and retrograde motion; their size and several prognostications; and other things which the reason of man had never discovered. There was also among them a philosopher well skilled in physic and natural philosophy, who asked the Lord Jesus, whether he had studied physic? He replied and explained to him physics and metaphysics. Also, those things which were above and below the power of nature; The powers also of the body, its humours, and their effects. Also the number of its members, and bones, veins, arteries, and nerves; The several constitutions of body, hot and dry, cold and moist, and the tendencies of them; How the soul operated upon the body; What its various sensations and faculties, were; The faculty of speaking, anger, desire; And lastly the manner of its composition and dissolution; and other things, which the understanding of no creature had ever reached. Then that philosopher arose, and worshipped the Lord Jesus, and said, O Lord Jesus, from henceforth I will be thy disciple and servant."
11

How is it that the poor carpenter's son from Nazareth we have all been told about was allowed entry into the temple by himself, much less given the floor to debate the temple elders? It doesn't make logical sense given the story we've been sold by the church. In their story, the Son of God is born to a virgin in a manger, appears for a brief moment at twelve years of age and then re-emerges to be baptized at the age of 30. Their story has caused many people to postulate why eighteen years of Jesus' life are missing from the record; some even saying it proves that Jesus never existed. It is true that eighteen years are missing from the record that the Bible's New Testament Gospels of Jesus provide to us. However, there are other gospels that never made it into the Bible, and they shed quite a bit of light on what Jesus was doing for all those years. In the following passage from The First Gospel of the Infancy of Jesus Christ, it says that Jesus was studying the law until he was thirty years old:

> CHAPTER XXII. 1 Jesus conceals his miracles, 2 <u>studies the law, 3 and is baptized. NOW from this time Jesus began to conceal his miracles and secret works, 2 And gave himself to the study of the law, till he arrived to the end of his thirtieth year;</u> 3 At which time the Father publicly owned him at Jordan, sending down this voice from heaven, This is my beloved son, in whom I am well pleased; 4 The Holy Ghost being also present in the form of a dove.[12]

If Jesus studied the law and was a Rabbi, then one can assume he was a Pharisee or Sadducee for all those years. This part of his history is not contained in the Bible and no preacher or religious teacher I have ever heard has ever made this point, which is absolutely shocking to me but not surprising based upon what happens after a mobbing has occurred. Personal histories are rewritten and legacies are stolen in order to support the false historical record that the perpetrators of the mobbing have created in order to achieve their goal of ridding their human target from their midst and justifying their behavior in the aftermath. In Jesus' case, he was painted as a fraud and impostor by the Jewish hierarchy, and as the literal son of God by the Christian community created by Paul. Paul had his own self-interested reasons for creating the only son of God narrative, which I detail in my book, *Patterns of Peter and Paul*. All I will say here is that Jesus set the stage for Paul with his own false narrative that I discuss later in this book. Unfortunately, mobbings often create this bevy of false narratives because all the participants in the mobbing, target and perpetrators alike, tell lies in an effort to protect themselves in the atmosphere of lies and deceit created by the mobbing itself.

Even though we know so little about Jesus' life, we can surmise from the passage above that the genius of Jesus was well known when he began teaching at 30 years of age. (See Matthew 3:11, Mark 1:7-8 and Luke 3:16) He had by that time attracted many educated people like the philosopher who became his servant and disciple after hearing him debate the chief priests in the temple while he was still a boy. Combine Jesus' superior intellect with his passion for truth and his unwillingness to compromise his beliefs and it was a tragedy waiting to happen in the corrupt temple workplace he was in. Criticizing any tight-knit group of people – particularly if it threatens their turf of power – is always a nebulous proposition.

Jesus was the light of truth among hypocrites and vipers spreading a false narrative. I talk in detail about their false doctrine in my other books and will not repeat it here except for reiterating Jesus' claim that he came to fulfill the law, not to abolish it. (Matthew 5:17) The law he came to fulfill is the law of truth. He came to fulfill the law of God who takes a stroll through the Garden of Eden and uncovers the falsehoods and lies of Man and Woman's egos. Jesus was trying to get them (and us) back on track from the kind of thinking represented by the Woman's encounter with the snake in the Garden. He was trying to get the Pharisees to change their focus from a reliance on the hundreds of laws contained within Mosaic Law to a reliance on the laws of their inner being. He was trying to get them to think in a new way that is as old as the Bible itself. He was trying to get them to repent.

Repentance is very hard when we have been raised by parents and teachers whose job it is to conform our thinking to a state where it will provide us with the means for our physical and financial survival within societal structures. Changing the state of our minds can mean the end of our survival within those structures if we find ourselves in a corrupt environment like Jesus found himself in.

4
Phase II: Mobbing and Stigmatizing
The Bullying Begins

Although adolescent bullying has never been studied from the viewpoint of mobbing, perhaps it should be since it usually follows the five phases of a mobbing identified by Leymann when it is not properly handled in the early stages. What we call bullying is usually initiated by one influential student in school who then rallies other students to his side based on a desire to get back at a classmate who has slighted the bully in some way. In my book, *The Evolution of Good and Evil*, I use the term 'power abuser' rather than bully because that is what a bully is. A bully is a person who has abused the power of his/her position as a human being by using the manipulation strategies inherent in the second phase of a mobbing. These strategies serve to change the image of the person they are targeting from good to bad in the eyes of others. Leymann identifies these five areas of manipulation as follows:

1. The target individual's good reputation is ruined through rumors, slander and lies;

2. Communications toward the target individual become hostile and all attempts by the target individual to be heard are blocked and/or denied;

3. The target individual is isolated from his colleagues;

4. The ability of the target individual to do his work is made impossible by either giving him no work or by giving him meaningless tasks; and

5. Violence or the threats of violence are directed against the target individual.

The second phase of a mobbing is called *the bullying and stigmatizing phase* because all the above strategies are used to objectify the targeted individual and make the bullied target into the instigator bully in the eyes of others. Only the orchestrators of the abuse – the real bullies and mobbers - are wise to what is actually being done, and they thoroughly enjoy watching as one employee, colleague and fellow student after another, whichever the case may be, fall into line joining in the abuse because it lets them know their strategy is working.

According to Leymann, this phase can last anywhere from days to years and it always has devastating effects on the targeted individual(s). For Jesus, it lasted just shy of three years – from the death of John the Baptist to Jesus' orchestrated crucifixion. The mock trial Jesus had to endure had witnesses who lied, conflicting testimony, and a blustering chief priest who played his part so well of displaying false indignation so brilliantly. Anyone who was in a position to help Jesus either hid or fell into line with the chief priest for fear of the same fate befalling them. (Matthew 26:57-68, Mark 14:53-65 and Luke 22:66-71) I dissect this trial line by line later on in the book when illustrating the power of group think in making us act against our better selves when the forces of power and control are exerted downward on us to conform or suffer the consequences. Suffice it to say here that Jesus was prosecuted and convicted solely on lies and some brilliant acting by the man at the top of the temple hierarchy who no one dared cross. No wonder Jesus stood in silence before Pilate. He knew there was nothing he could say or do to save himself against people who would lie, harass, trick, deceive and manipulate any situation to achieve their desired goal of eliminating Jesus from their workplace and lives.

The New Testament of the Bible does not introduce us to Jesus until he has been isolated and made an outcast by his Pharisaic colleagues in this second phase. The missing eighteen years of his life when he was studying the law to become a rabbi and priest are not addressed at all in the four gospels of Jesus found in the Books of Matthew, Mark, Luke and John. Nor is there any mention of those missing years in the rest of the New Testament largely authored by the self-labeled apostle Paul, who was likely a fellow student and colleague of Jesus given the fact they were the same age and both students of the law. Who knows? He could even have been the Pharisee who got triggered given his propensity for hunting down and killing the followers of Jesus before his alleged *miraculous vision* on the road to Damascus. (See Acts 7:54-60, Acts 8:1-3, and Acts 9:1-9)

But I digress. What the four gospels of Jesus do give us is a fairly detailed case study of a workplace mobbing, along with some great insights into what a targeted individual should and should not do to protect against the devastating psychological, emotional and financial toll that mobbings take on targeted individuals like Leif and other workers and students in our workplaces and schools.

Jesus' interactions with the Pharisees serve as a case study for what Leymann identifies as the five areas of manipulation used during the stigmatizing phase of a mobbing. The motive for using these tactics of manipulation is to convince coworkers and managers that the targeted individual deserves the abuse to which he/she is being subjected.

As already pointed out, the typical target is usually well liked and a valued member of the organization who, for various reasons, finds him/herself in the crosshairs of someone who wants them gone. It is very hard, if not impossible, to get people to attack someone they value and like. Therefore, that reality needs to be turned upside-down if the aggressor/power abuser is to achieve his goals. The well-liked and valued member of the organization has to somehow become devalued in the eyes of other people so that their opinions of the target change and give them justification for participating in the gang-style mobbing the aggressor wants to orchestrate. This changing of reality is done by manipulating the truth. Manipulating the truth about the targeted individual's true character is the motive behind the five tactics of manipulation Leymann identified.

Although Christianity has done its own manipulation of truth to create an image of Jesus that supports the religion, the facts remain for anyone to see. Jesus was targeted by the Pharisees because someone wanted him gone and they used the strategies of the mob identified for us by Leymann to achieve their goal.

Mob Strategy No. 1: Reputation manipulation

Reputation manipulation is a nice way of saying character assassination. Don't you think it is time to analyze how a popular healer and teacher like Jesus came to be an enemy of the state who posed a national security risk? (See John 11:49-50) How could it happen that his self-righteous Pharisee colleagues felt justified in kicking, hitting, whipping and spitting upon him before sending him to a horrible torture they were responsible for initiating? (Matthew 27:67, Mark 14:65 and John 18:22)

What I found is that it was the same process that transformed Leif from a skillful and competent worker to an unemployable outcast with mental and emotional issues. This process of image reversal through character assassination is outlined in stunning detail in the New Testament Gospels of Jesus. All it takes is a change in how we have historically perceived these gospels; due to the intractable doctrine of the Christian Church.

Leymann says that rumor mongering, slander and ridicule are used to besmirch the targeted individual's character. According to the following passages in Matthew, Jesus was a satanic, gluttonous, alcoholic in the eyes of the Pharisees:

> Matthew 9:32-34 and Matthew 12:22-37: "As they were going out, a demoniac who could not speak was brought to him and when the demon was driven out the mute person spoke. The crowds were amazed and said, "Nothing like this has ever been seen in Israel. But the Pharisees said, "He drives out demons by the prince of demons."
>
> Matthew 11:19 and Luke 7:34: "The Son of Man came eating and drinking and they said, "Look, he is a glutton and a drunkard, a friend of tax collectors and sinners."

The Pharisees are power abusers who not only don't want to give Jesus credit for his amazing abilities, they want to degrade him and his abilities in the eyes of others. They are the same authoritarian type leaders as the men in Leif's factory who felt entitled to denigrating Leif's abilities and talents to anyone who would listen and sent him on false missions to make it look like he was incompetent. The people who engage in these malicious tactics know what they are doing and as much as we like to deny it, they thoroughly enjoy the game. They know the harm they are inflicting, but they get a kick out of watching the results because it feeds their need for revenge at what they themselves perceive as an injustice.

In Leif's case, his abilities and talents earned him a higher salary and his less skilled colleagues were jealous. In Jesus' case, the resentment and hatred the Pharisees felt towards him for showing them to be the hypocrites and snakes they were fueled their desire for revenge. Instead of dealing with their feelings of injustice constructively, they used a conscious strategy to gain the upper hand and destroy their prey. Throughout the four Gospels of Jesus, the

Pharisees are right there hounding and belittling Jesus and his teachings. When their strategies didn't work and Jesus gained a huge following in spite of all their ridicule and marginalization tactics, they instituted a strategy of elimination.

The Pharisees who accused Jesus of Satanism knew they were lying and didn't care because they wanted to undermine him. (See Matthew 12:22-25) Their motive was malevolent and done to harm the reputation of another human being. However, to an outsider who was not aware of their malevolence, they could have appeared to have a valid point. Jesus was working with a largely uneducated public that looked to the Pharisees for direction and leadership. They accepted what their elders told them without doing the work of determining for themselves whether Jesus was satanic or not. It goes back to the Bully-Enabler-Bystander-Target model of behavior that I discuss in *The Evolution of Good and Evil*. There are people who are consciously evil (the power abusers of our world) and there are people who help them or merely stand by for fear of becoming the next target if they speak up (the enablers and bystanders).

Our ego-centered morality that focuses on what we do comes in very handy for corrupt power abusers. Jesus did not have the credentials of the Pharisee leadership. He was not a member of the good 'ol boy temple network who held positions and titles that made people perceive them as righteous men of God. Jesus was off doing his own thing, so it was very easy to paint him as the oddball Satan follower opposing the righteous men of God.

Power abusers like Caiaphas and the Pharisees can always create an image of righteousness that covers up their motives for doing what they do. Caiaphas was not only not punished for the harassment and intended murder of Jesus, he consolidated his power with further lies and intimidation against the disciples who sought to follow in Jesus' footsteps. In the Book of Acts, we meet Caiaphas once again when Peter and John appear before him to answer for healing a man through applying what Jesus taught them. After voicing his amazement that such uneducated and ignorant men could do such things (which is how many extremely egocentric and schooled people view people without a higher education), Caiaphas wants them killed. The only reason they were not killed was because the Sanhedrin's equivalent of what we would today refer to as a chief ethics officer and general counsel tells him to hold on. Gamaliel, a teacher in the law, provides an alternative strategy for handling the situation telling the members of the Sanhedrin:

> So in the present case, I tell you, keep away from these men and let them alone; because if this plan or this undertaking is of human origin, it will fail; but if it is of God, you will not be able to overthrow them—in that case you may even be found fighting against God!"

It is not surprising to me that a few short chapters later we are introduced to a Pharisee named Saul who experiences a miraculous conversion and begins focusing his followers on the "do" of their behavior with all the do's and don'ts I learned in the Baptist Church of my youth. Not coincidentally, Saul was trained in the law under Gamaliel. (Acts 22:3) That education made him very successful in making the message 'of human origin' rather than of God by placing the focus on a physical man sent to die by the guy in the sky so he could cancel out the sin committed by the physical guy made by God in the Garden of Eden. It was very much an eye for an eye, a tooth for a tooth kind of philosophy that the gentile congregations of Paul's churches were very familiar with.

Paul created the ridiculous doctrine I rejected as a teenager which bears no resemblance to the awareness teachings of Jesus Christ. He reinforced the notion of an all-powerful and all-loving God in the sky who has the power of stopping bad stuff from ever happening to us here on earth but for some reason chooses not to. He annihilated the awareness teachings of Jesus and it has taken us

2,000+ years to gain back any ground in the area of our minds and their ability to move mountains when the energy of faith within ourselves is activated.

Corrupted minds like those of the Pharisees who harassed Jesus and tried to destroy his reputation do not see their actions as wrong. They see themselves as upstanding citizens and high-achieving pillars of the community. I personally believe this is why corruption is as old as the human species itself. People with pharisaic minds are incapable of following Jesus's commandment to Nicodemus to look inward because they do not see the need. They are positioned well within society and that is a very comfortable place to be. They are not interested in self-awareness and truth if it threatens to get in the way of the image they so carefully cultivate for presentation to the world.

The Pharisees know exactly what they are doing in trying to destroy Jesus' reputation but they feel quite justified in degrading his accomplishments to the crowds because Jesus is stealing some of the thunder they feel they deserve by right of their positions and titles. The Pharisees couldn't care less about maintaining the integrity of the Temple that provided them their livelihoods. Their loyalty was to themselves and retaining the tassels on their robes that gave them instant respect and authority within the community without having to earn it. Jesus said, "All their works are performed to be seen. They widen their phylacteries and lengthen their tassels. They love places of honor at banquets, seats of honor in synagogues, greeting in marketplaces and the salutation 'Rabbi.'" (Matthew 23:5-6) The Temple itself was superfluous to them. It was just a means to the end of providing them with what they considered their just rewards because of the label they had been given as priestly experts in the law.

Unlike Leif who responded to his colleagues' manipulations and deceit with anger, Jesus always responded to the attacks of his Pharisee accusers with logic and humor. It was not until he became aware that he was a wanted man that he became aggressive and threw the money changers out of the temple. Perhaps it is because of Jesus' composure and single-minded focus on his work and mission that we have failed to realize the maliciousness of the campaign that was waged against him. When I read the New Testament Gospels of Jesus now, I am acutely aware of how Jesus was undermined by a group of Pharisee colleagues who were jealous of him and never gave him a second's rest from their spying eyes and manipulations.

I am also very cognizant of how their strategies to destroy Jesus financially, mentally, emotionally and physically were no different than the mobbing and bullying strategies used today. The Pharisees were always trying to entrap Jesus by getting him to say something so they could arrest him. When this strategy of entrapment is used in the workplace, its purpose is to get the targeted employee terminated for insubordination. Insubordination is a quick and effective way for higher-ups to rid themselves of subordinates they have labeled as troublemakers. When it comes to interpersonal conflict in the workplace, it is usually one person's word against another person's word. In cases of insubordination, the default winner in a he-said, she-said situation is usually the person at the higher level of the organization.

Here are a couple exchanges the Pharisees had with Jesus in their attempts to entrap him into saying something blasphemous so they could arrest him. I think these are among my favorite passages because they provide a glimpse into the man that Jesus was.

> Matthew 21:23-27: And when he was come into the temple, the chief priests and the elders of the people came unto him as he was teaching, and said, By what authority doest thou these things? and who gave thee this authority? And Jesus answered and said unto them, I also will ask you one question, which if ye tell me, I likewise will tell you by what authority I do these things.

The baptism of John, whence was it? from heaven or from men? And they reasoned with themselves, saying, If we shall say, From heaven; he will say unto us, Why then did ye not believe him? But if we shall say, From men; we fear the multitude; for all hold John as a prophet. And they answered Jesus, and said, We know not. He also said unto them, Neither tell I you by what authority I do these things.

Matthew 22:15-22: They watched him closely and sent agents pretending to be righteous who were to trap him in speech, in order to hand him over to the authority and power of the governor. They posed this question to him, "Teacher, we know that what you say and teach is correct, and you show no partiality, but teach the way of God in accordance with the truth. Is it lawful for us to pay tribute to Caesar or not?" Recognizing their craftiness he said to them, "Show me a denarius; whose image and name does it bear?" They replied, "Caesar's." So he said to them, "Then repay to Caesar what belongs to Caesar and to God what belongs to God." They were unable to trap him by something he might say before the people, and so amazed were they at his reply that they fell silent.

In the second passage above, the Pharisees have sent some of their disciples to ask Jesus if it is lawful to pay the census tax to Caesar. They probably sat around for hours coming up with that question, reasoning that if Jesus said 'yes' it would make his followers, who already felt they were overtaxed by the Roman army, angry at him. But if Jesus said 'no' it would make the government angry at him. No doubt, they were certain that they finally put Jesus in the proverbial no-win situation. It is every power abuser's dream come true!

Look at how they set up the question. They are all so pleasant and polite, acting as if they are truly interested in what he has to say. I can just picture them smiling at Jesus and maybe even slightly bowing in deference to him as they ask: "Teacher, we know that you are a truthful man and that you teach the way of God in accordance with the truth. And you are not concerned with anyone's opinion, for you do not regard a person's status. Tell us, then, what is your opinion: Is it lawful to pay the census tax to Caesar or not?"

I love how Jesus replies. He sees right through them and knows exactly what they are trying to do with this question. "Why are you testing me, you hypocrites?" he asks them. Jesus never minced words. I can almost hear the agitation in his voice as begins to turn the tables on them and says, "Show me the coin that pays the tax." As they hand it to him, he takes it, holds it up and asks them: "Whose image is this and whose inscription?" They have no choice but to say "Ceasar's," to which Jesus tells them "then repay to Caesar what belongs to Caesar and to God what belongs to God." There had to have been some cheering going on at the sheer genius of that reply. The story ends by saying that the men who asked the question were amazed and left without saying anything in response.

Even though Jesus was able to see right through them and knew what they were doing, not everyone has that ability. The chief priests who approached Jesus were charmers. They appeared to be truly sincere and interested in what Jesus had to say. I have no doubt their charming demeanor worked in their favor on their respective climbs to the top of the hierarchy. They were living, breathing examples of how the appearance of truth, rather than truth itself, can work in one's favor in too many instances. They were like the charmer of a husband who everyone adores, but behind closed doors makes it a habit of beating his wife. The wife knows what a monster she is married to but has quit telling anyone else because they are unable to see past the facade he puts on in front of them. The chief priests were also like school bullies who are popular and well-liked, but have used the strategies of the mob to turn their targets into outcasts who the teachers and principal perceive as loners who bring the problems on themselves by not trying to fit in.

People like the Pharisees who harassed Jesus usually get away with their actions with their reputations intact because the rest of us do not want to believe that people who appear to be so charming, popular and well-liked can, at the same time, be so manipulative, deceitful and cruel. The Pharisees who approached Jesus appeared to be truly sincere. To any outsider witnessing the interaction, it certainly would have appeared as if they were truly interested in what Jesus had to say. Little would they know that the vipers, hypocrites and snakes had carefully planned each of these encounters as a means of entrapping Jesus in his speech so they could arrest him on charges of blasphemy.

The strategies of reputation destruction through deceit, entrapment, secrecy and lies are as old as mankind itself. The only thing that changes is our perception of the people who use them and the people they are used against. This game of perception makes us think in terms of good guys vs. bad guys, good vs. evil. In this game, unfortunately, it is usually the players with more power and greater means at their disposal for manipulating information in their favor who win and come out on top appearing as the good guys in the equation..

Instead of viewing morality as good vs. evil (good guys vs. bad guys) we should become detectives in the workings of the human mind. We should begin identifying patterns of thought that cause the human mind to become corrupted. We should attempt to identify and isolate tactics like those used by the Pharisees to destroy a human being who has done nothing wrong so that we can nullify their effectiveness through knowledge and awareness.

Although I do not condone their actions, I totally understand where the Pharisee mob was coming when they went after Jesus. They looked at him as the enemy who was humiliating them and putting their doctrine and behavior to shame. When the leaders of their temple hierarchy backed them in their campaign of bullying against Jesus, they felt even more justified in their cruelty.

I think that is where Jesus miscalculated. He miscalculated the power of the structure. Although he was aware of the low character of the men themselves, I am not sure he was aware of the space (network) they were operating in. God's space bends. The network of the hierarchy does not allow for any bending. It is static and hard. There is no room for alternate structures or ideas. Jesus' knowledge of human nature and his application of that knowledge to his life and experience could only take him so far within that structure until the inevitable hammer came down on him – as it eventually comes down on all dissenters who threaten world views upon which these hierarchies of power depend.

Mob Strategy No. 2: Hostile communications

Leymann describes Mob Strategy No. 2 as a hostile attempt to silence the targeted individuals with actions like loud-voiced criticism, meaningful facial expressions and putting up outright barriers that serve to keep their voices from being heard. Sometimes, the communications do not even have to be direct to be hostile. A condescending eye roll, sneer or look of disgust can do the job even better.

Jesus was subjected to a barrage of criticism from the Pharisees in their attempt to destroy him and his teachings. Most of the time it was verbal, but there were some instances where the hostility was much more subtle. In one such instance, Jesus is sitting at table with his disciples when some tax collectors and other people the Pharisees considered sinners join them. When the Pharisees see Jesus with these people, they ask his disciples (not him) why he is sitting with such people – the implication being they never would. (Matthew 9:9-12, Mark 2:15-16)

When I was a church goer, this scene was always presented as an illustration of Jesus' compassion for the hurt and wounded among society's outcasts. We are never asked to take a look at that scene from the perspective of what it means in terms of class. Here we have Jesus, an expert in the law just as his Pharisee colleagues are, and he is sitting among the people perceived as sinners by the Pharisees, while the Pharisees are sitting together at a different table mocking him. They presented themselves as leaders of the Jewish people and yet they are mocking the only one among them who is actually making himself accessible to the people. They were like modern-day managers, executives and CEOs of companies who present themselves as leaders of their organizations, but who themselves have never worked on a shop floor or store aisle their entire careers. Worse yet, they feel it degrading to leave the perches of their corporate offices to spend any time on the floor to learn more about the work their subordinates do day-in and day-out to make their paychecks and bonuses so large. When was the last time you saw a CEO who is complaining about the lack of workers available to pick fruit in the fields who himself is willing to go out there and pick it? It has never happened and never will happen because of the class strata that puts him in a corporate executive suite box and his fruit pickers in a laborer's sweat shop box.

Part and parcel with their hostile communications towards Jesus was the Pharisees' use of the laws they were experts in to silence and destroy a man whose every word and action was guided by the laws of God. Funny how the law always seemed to be on their side in these instances. In one particular encounter which I give below, Jesus has decided to cure a man on the Sabbath despite being told it was against the law to do any work on the Sabbath. Like so many doctors and healers today who use effective therapies to treat and even cure diseases of their suffering patients only to end up on the enemies list of the hierarchy of the American Medical

Association which doesn't approve of their approaches,[13] the Pharisees immediately went out and began planning how to destroy Jesus:

> "Departing from there, He went into their synagogue. And a man *was there* whose hand was withered. And they questioned Jesus, asking, "Is it lawful to heal on the Sabbath?"—so that they might accuse Him. And He said to them, "What man is there among you who has a sheep, and if it falls into a pit on the Sabbath, will he not take hold of it and lift it out? How much more valuable then is a man than a sheep! So then, it is lawful to do good on the Sabbath." <u>Then He said to the man, "Stretch out your hand!" He stretched it out, and it was restored to normal, like the other. But the Pharisees went out and conspired against Him, *as to* how they might destroy Him."</u> (Matthew 12:9-14)

These verses provide a wonderful example of how corrupt political types like the Pharisees will follow the letter of the law to get someone they want out of the way. We are told that laws, policies, rules and procedures are put into place to protect us. However, when we lose sight of the spirit of those laws, policies, rules and procedures in our desire to destroy another human being, we lose our humanity. Jesus could have cured this man on any other day of the week and he would have been safe from the prosecutorial eyes of the Pharisees. However, since Jesus cured the man on the Sabbath it gave the Pharisees the ammunition they needed because the law on the books said no work was to be done on the Sabbath.

In cases like this, laws and policies that are rarely, if ever, used against anyone else, are used as a quick and easy way to take care of people labeled as troublemakers, dissenters, whistleblowers and enemies of the state. As Jesus so rightly points out to them, they are applying the law so strictly with him even though the Pharisees wouldn't hesitate to work at getting their sheep out of a pit if it fell into it on the Sabbath. In addition to insubordination, this is another favorite tactic of workplaces to get rid of troublesome employees. They will dust off their employee manuals and policy rule books in their effort to apply a rule that has never been applied to anyone else before for purposes of terminating the employee.

Mob Strategy No. 3: Isolation

Like Leif, the factory worker, targeted individuals like Jesus are left out there on their own because their persecutors have maliciously and with intent put them out there on their own through isolation and the other strategies of the mob; while the persecutors themselves remain safe and beyond reproach hidden as they are behind the facades they so carefully craft for the general public. Perhaps what prevented Jesus from suffering the overwhelming feelings of isolation that most victims of mobbing suffer was the network of supporters he built in the form of his disciples. Even though the Pharisees denied him a seat at their own table and were critical of him for sitting with tax collectors, Jesus was able to retain his sense of confidence because he had supporters both within his own circle of friends and disciples, as well as within the general population.

Ironically, one of Jesus' strongest supporters was a Pharisee named Nicodemus. We are told in John 3:1 that Nicodemus is a ruler of the Jews who approaches Jesus at night wanting to talk to him. The New Testament account does not indicate when this conversation took place or whether it was the first conversation Nicodemus ever had with Jesus. What we do know is that Nicodemus, unlike his fellow Pharisees who ridiculed and harassed Jesus, became very close to Jesus at some point in time because he was one of four people who laid claim to Jesus' body after the crucifixion. It also says in the *Apocryphal Gospel of Nicodemus* that the "unjust Jews" went after Nicodemus for showing kindness towards Jesus:

> "The Jews angry with Nicodemus: and with, Joseph of Arimathaea, whom they imprison. When the unjust Jews heard that Joseph had begged and buried the body of Jesus, they sought after Nicodemus, and those fifteen men who had testified before the governor, that Jesus was not born through fornication, and other good persons who had shown any good actions towards him. But when they all concealed themselves through fear of the Jews, Nicodemus alone showed himself to them, and said, How can such persons as these enter into the synagogue?"[14]

I believe the conversation between Jesus and Nicodemus found in John, Chapter 3, was most likely the first time the two men met face- to-face. I do not believe, however, that it was Nicodemus' intent to befriend Jesus at the meeting. When he approaches Jesus, he tells him,

> "Rabbi, we know that You have come from God as a teacher; for no one can do these signs that You do unless God is with him." (John 3:2)

As pleasant as this greeting sounds, I think it indicates a different and far more likely motive than friendship. The Pharisees hated Jesus. Throughout the four Gospels of Jesus, it is clear that the only reason they ever spoke to Jesus was to get him to say something they could use against him in order to arrest him. (See Matthew 12:10, Matthew 21:45-46, Matthew 26:3-5, Mark 14:1-2, Luke 6:9-11) The greeting Nicodemus gives to Jesus mirrors the greeting made to Jesus in Matthew 22:15-18, where the Pharisee leadership tries to get Jesus to say that Jews shouldn't pay their taxes, for the sole purpose of arresting him and getting him charged with an executable crime under Roman law. That greeting reads as follows:

"Teacher, we know that You are truthful and teach the way of God in truth, and defer to no one; for You are not partial to any. Tell us then, what do You think? Is it lawful to give a poll-tax to Caesar, or not?"

The similarity in the tone of Nicodemus' greeting to that of the Pharisee agents sent to trick Jesus certainly seems to affirm that Nicodemus may have been a player in the same strategy to get Jesus to say something worthy of arrest. No doubt Nicodemus heard all the malicious gossip about how Jesus drank too much and was a glutton. (Matthew 11:19) When Nicodemus finally got the chance to talk to this fat, drunken prophet spouting a ludicrous message of self-awareness and repentance, he was no doubt prepared to ridicule him as his colleagues so often did to make themselves appear superior in front of everyone. If his intention was to get Jesus to say something worthy of arrest, he may even have relished his role in being the one they chose to do it. Whatever his intention was in personally seeking out Jesus, I am quite certain Nicodemus was not prepared to have his world turned right side up and his belief system flipped on its ear by a wise and insightful teacher who saw through all the hypocrisy and rationalizations that had become a way of life for Nicodemus and his cohorts in power. When Nicodemus spoke to Jesus one-on-one with no one else around, it gave him the opportunity to really listen to what Jesus was teaching, unfiltered by all the gossip and misrepresentations he heard from his fellow Pharisees. The conversation that ensued between the two men made Nicodemus a believer; not in a crucified Jesus but in a God that Jesus made real to him with his words. Jesus gave Nicodemus something that the laws of the temple never could – a glimpse at reality.

Jesus responds to Nicodemus' initial greeting by telling him the reason he can do what he does is because he understands the truth about his own existence in consciousness - what Jesus always referred to as the spirit of the Father within. When Jesus tells Nicodemus he needs to change his focus from adhering to the set of external laws known as Mosaic Law and begin listening to the law of his inner being (become born again), Nicodemus is completely lost. He even asks him, "How can a man be born when he is old? He cannot enter a second time into his mother's womb and be born, can he?" (John 3:4) This sounds like a stupid question and Nicodemus is definitely not a stupid man. Rather, he is a man trying to understand a concept that is completely foreign to him as someone who has risen through the ranks of the temple hierarchy. It would be like speaking French to a classroom of English-speaking students. Nicodemus has no frame of reference for what Jesus is telling him. He has spent his life using his brain to memorize and follow the 600+ laws contained within Mosaic Law that cover all aspects of personal conduct, grooming and thought. When Jesus uses the metaphor of birth to describe the process of transforming from a brain following laws to a mind experiencing its own life force, it is only natural that Nicodemus would miss the subtlety of the metaphor and ask how a person already born can go back into the mother's womb and be born again.

Nicodemus is like so many of us raised in societies where we are taught to do what our parents, teachers, bosses and other authoritarian figures tell us. He knew the letter of the law without having any knowledge of the spirit of the law. He knew what he was taught but he had no knowledge of himself. Nicodemus was a doer without the knowledge of why he was doing it. It is natural that he would take Jesus' words literally. That is what rules like laws do. They train us to follow them without giving us the rationale or reason behind them. If common sense gets in the way of the law, then the hammer comes down to bring us back into conformance or face the consequences. Each time we are brought back into conformance by our parents, teachers, bosses, government, police and other agents of authority we learn to suppress our own judgment in favor of following a dictated course of action that we know will not get us in trouble. Society's rules, social mores and customs become the standard by which we gauge our behavior – good and bad – and society's rules include religious doctrine. It doesn't take long to figure out that if we want to escape punishment for going against the rules, then we need to either find a way around the rules or take our chances getting caught for breaking them.

Nicodemus had his feet so firmly planted in conforming to society's standards and laws that even as a supposed man of God, he was unable to experience God. He had a brain trained to do the work of God, but he had no idea how to be godlike. The idea that God was Nicodemus' own consciousness (spirit within) was out in the land of loony tunes for a practical man like Nicodemus who viewed God as a guy in the sky who is keeping track of everything we do and every law we break. His doctrine had separated him from his true existence by placing the focus on his external behavior; so much so that when Jesus tried to explain to him a concept existing in mind, he was unable to fathom it.

Being born again is not a one-time declaration of accepting Jesus as our Lord and Savior as Christian doctrine tells us. According to Jesus, it is a moment-by-moment state of being. It must be because it is a process of the mind. We are born again every time we replace the thought that we are unworthy of happiness with the thought that we are made of spirit, and our true natural state is one of joy and peace. We are born again every time we make a difficult choice that may be painful in the short-term but is the right course of action in the long-term to ensure the well-being of ourselves and others. We are born again each time we realize that something we have said or done is wrong (not in alignment with a consciousness of truth) and we decide to apologize and, if necessary, change the behavior. We are born again when we do not allow ourselves to sink into self-pity and depression when faced with difficult circumstances. We are born again when we follow a courageous course of action that may cause us to suffer material loss in the short-term but does not compromise our long-term growth and evolution. We are born again when we apply self-discipline to breaking a bad habit. We are born again every time we make the conscious decision to improve ourselves in some area of our life, or when we do something to improve another person's life.

Nicodemus was living a great life before his talk with Jesus. He was a leader of the community. He had it all, or so he thought, until he had his talk with Jesus. Jesus awakened the voice of truth within him that had long been silent. He had accepted the physical world as the reality of his existence and thereby limited his perceptions of that world to a brain that accepted the parameters that other men created for him over time to navigate within. Breaking out of those parameters became almost as detrimental to Nicodemus as they became for Jesus. Questioning authority and resisting conformity always comes with consequences. It is a hard road to follow because it can be very harmful to our way of life and result in a spanking, a bad grade on a test, loss of a job, alienation from our peers, imprisonment or worse. It requires a great deal of courage to follow a consciousness of truth but once the commitment is made, the thought of returning to a state of ignorance is repugnant.

I believe that Nicodemus approached Jesus in the darkness of night because it was his dark intent to trick him. What happened instead is that he went away a devoted friend who put his own life on the line to help Jesus in his darkest hours. I never heard of Nicodemus before I actually decided to read the Bible for myself and have since come to admire and respect him so much. I think it may have been Nicodemus of whom Jesus was thinking when he told his disciples at the last supper, "Greater love hath no man than this, that a man lay down his life for his friends." (John 15:13) The kind of love that Nicodemus had for Jesus and Jesus had for him is the kind of love that all men and women would have for one another in a world grounded in the reality of truth where our connection to one another would be as natural as the structures created by an animal consciousness has made our disconnection.

Mob Strategy No. 4: No work and/or meaningless tasks given to targeted individual

Jesus was a rabbi without tassels. After he made the decision to give up the law in favor of becoming a teacher and healer, he was out there on his own. Although *The First Gospel of the Infancy of Jesus Christ* indicates he was studying the law until the age of 30, the New Testament Gospels do not introduce us to Jesus until after he has achieved the title of Rabbi. His entire history from the age of 12 until the age of 30 has been wiped from the official record known as the Bible. I am quite certain we would never have heard of Jesus at all if he had not been smart and strategic. Just like John the Baptist before him, Jesus had many disciples. But unlike John, Jesus chose twelve of those disciples to personally mentor. Jesus was very much aware of the circumstances of John's death and he was acutely aware that the Pharisees were out for him. By choosing twelve disciples to mentor, he held a better chance of preserving his teachings after he was gone.

In one documentary I saw recently, the producer/director makes the claim that Jesus never existed and backs up his claim with examples of mythological gods who all had twelve disciples.[15] For an example, he uses Horus, the sun god of Egypt. Horus was born on December 25, his birth was accompanied by a star in the east, he had twelve disciples, he performed miracles and he was dead for three days before being resurrected. Likewise, the stories are the same for Krishna of India, Dionysus of Greece and Mithra of Persia.[16]

It is true they all had twelve disciples, but I would say in the case of Jesus, choosing twelve disciples was a strategic move made with the intention to shift the balance of power from Caiaphas and the mob to him.

Jesus was acutely aware that the Pharisees were out for him. After Jesus cured a man in the temple on the Sabbath despite being told it was against the law to do any work on the Sabbath, the Pharisees immediately went out and began planning how to destroy him. (Matthew 12:13-14) In the following verse in Matthew, it says that when Jesus found out their intentions, he left that town and continued curing people wherever he went; always warning them not to tell anybody.

I always thought it was Jesus' humility that made him advise people not to tell, but that wasn't it at all. It was a matter of self-preservation. That was also the reason he spoke in parables. It wasn't because he wanted us to guess at what he was saying. I think Jesus, being the logical seeker of truth that he was, would have loved to have been able to come out and say what he meant as clearly as possible so that it was not open to interpretation as it is today. But he could not. Everywhere he went there were Pharisees around him trying to find the slightest reason to arrest him for blasphemy. They would have loved for him to say that God is our own spirit of life within, so they could pin a charge of blasphemy on him by equating himself to God. A charge of blasphemy was useful in destroying anyone whose speech threatened them or their rule over the Jewish community. It was also a very effective way to derail any Messiah that Jewish prophets like Isaiah had predicted was coming.

Since Jesus' story and history is the same as these mythological figures, the director concludes that Jesus is a myth as well. Since I look at the world through the same rational lens that the director does, I would probably make the same conclusion if my world view did not include personal knowledge of the effects that bullying and mobbing have on the human psyche.

Rationally, mythological gods are just that – mythological. Make-believe characters can be made to do anything. If Jesus was a mythological god, then he could be made to rise from the dead. However, if he was a real man, that would be an impossible feat. Physical beings are restrained by the physical laws of nature while they inhabit this physical planet and one of those laws is that death is irreversible. You are either dead or you are not. There is no coming back from it and if you do come back, you were never dead to begin with.

If Jesus was a real man, rather than a myth, then (1) he either died on the cross and his disciples and other witnesses made up the story of seeing him alive afterward, (2) he survived the cross and lived to tell about it, or (3) his story is fiction and he never existed. Those are the only three possibilities in the world of matter in which we live. I personally believe Jesus was a real man who existed 2,000+ years ago because even though many gods have the same mythologized structure as Jesus, mythological gods do not have such detailed teachings penned by so many different people. The philosophy of Jesus is spelled out in the Gospels of Jesus contained in the New Testament of the Bible, in the newly discovered writings contained in the Nag Hammadi and Dead Sea Scrolls and, I am certain, in many other scrolls and codices buried deep underground that are yet to be discovered – including the underground of the Vatican. And since it is a physical impossibility for a real person to bodily come back from the dead, I do not believe Jesus ever died. A person must give up all reason, logic and knowledge of science to believe otherwise. I also do not believe the disciples made up the story because the disciples themselves expressed doubt about whether what they were seeing was true. (Matthew 28:17, Mark 16:14, Luke 24:37-39, John 20:24-28) If they made the story up, we would never have the expression 'a doubting Thomas' because there would have been no reason for them to express doubt. The other reason I do not believe the story was made up is because of the precision with which events played out to match the prophesies of Isaiah and it was Jesus who was always the one to point out these similarities to his disciples so that they would remember them after he was gone.

After Caiaphas met with the Pharisees and chief priests and the decision was made to kill Jesus, the Bible says, "Jesus therefore walked no more openly among the Jews; but went thence unto a country near to the wilderness, into a city called Ephraim, and there continued with his disciples." (John 11:54) Jesus did not attend council meetings, so how did he know that it would be smart not to walk openly among the Jews? I think it was because he was privy to what was being discussed in Caiaphas' and the Council's closed-door meetings.

This verse is the first indication that Jesus was receiving information from the inside about what the Council was planning for him. I believe two of the disciples who kept their discipleship secret from the Pharisees and who were attending those council meetings were Joseph of Arimathea and Nicodemus.[17] Both these men were the ones to claim Jesus' body after the crucifixion and take him to the tomb. In Luke 23:50-51, Joseph of Arimathea is described as a virtuous and righteous man who, though a member of the Council, had not consented to their plan of action. Nicodemus is similarly described as a ruler of the Jews. (John 3:1) Both men held positions that would have had them attending Council meetings and hearing everything Caiaphas said.

His foreknowledge of events made available to him by his friends on the Council is made crystal clear right before his arrest takes place in John 18. As Judas arrives with soldiers, Jesus is there to meet them because he already knows they are coming. Verse four says, "Jesus therefore, knowing all things that should come upon him, went forth, and said unto them, Whom seek ye?" (John 18:7)

I believe when Jesus heard of Caiaphas' intent to kill him

from Joseph of Arimathea, Nicodemus and possibly other secret followers on the Council, he went into survival mode. It would have been natural for him because he was a realist who constantly examined himself to ensure that everything he did was aligned with his two greatest commandments: "Thou shalt love the Lord thy God with all thy heart, and with all thy soul, and with all thy mind, and with all thy strength: and thou shalt love thy neighbour as thyself. There is none other commandment greater than these." (Matthew 22:36-40, Mark 12:28-31)

Loving God with all your heart, soul, mind and strength requires you to protect yourself. We are God's consciousness on this planet. It is a person's solemn obligation to express that consciousness by looking at all situations rationally and realistically, particularly when one's views conflict with the irrational and vindictive nature of authoritarian leaders who seek to maintain control at the personal expense of the people they control. Jesus wanted to control his own destiny. He did not want to end up like John the Baptist with his head on a platter. Saving himself and his teachings required him to be strategic and remain one step ahead of the Pharisee leadership who made it clear they would settle for nothing less than his head. It is my belief that Jesus worked out the only viable solution he felt he had in order to both stay alive and keep his message alive.

If Jesus was the Messiah, as I believe he was and as much of the Jewish community was beginning to believe he was, then why not reinforce that belief by aligning actions with what the Pharisees expected to see in a Messiah? Wouldn't that shift the balance of power in a way that would protect Jesus physically and reinforce his legacy as the teacher from Nazareth who showed the Jews how to free themselves from the yoke of tyranny imposed upon them by the Pharisaic hierarchy and the Roman state by freeing their minds of the same lies Nicodemus had such a hard time freeing himself from due to his lack of knowledge and understanding. This strategy makes perfect sense, particularly since the Pharisees asked him on several occasions for a sign he was the Messiah. They loved supernatural signs and wonders as much as so many Christians today do.

The Pharisees were always asking Jesus for a sign he was the Messiah. Below are just two examples:

Matthew 16:1-4: "The Pharisees and Sadducees came up, and testing Jesus, they asked Him to show them a sign from heaven. But He replied to them, "When it is evening, you say, 'It will be fair weather, for the sky is red.' And in the morning, 'There will be a storm today, for the sky is red and threatening.' Do you know how to discern the appearance of the sky, but cannot discern the signs of the times? An evil and adulterous generation seeks after a sign; and a sign will not be given it, except the sign of Jonah." And He left them and went away."

Matthew 12:38-40: "Then some of the scribes and Pharisees said to Him, "Teacher, we want to see a sign from You." But He answered and said to them, "An evil and adulterous generation craves for a sign; and yet no sign will be given to it but the sign of Jonah the prophet; for just as Jonah was three days and three nights in the belly of the sea monster, so will the Son of Man be three days and three nights in the heart of the earth."

Like many modern-day Christians, the Pharisees were great believers in signs from God. [See Acts 23:8] I think Jesus used those beliefs to try to save his teachings. I think he reasoned that he would bolster his teachings by giving the Pharisees the kind of supernatural sign we would expect from a guy in the sky operating in a physical universe. Jesus could have reasoned that if he gave the Pharisees what he believed would be a convincing sign he was the Messiah, it would support everything he had said and done up to that point and they might quit harassing him. What Jesus may have failed to know or consider was that their motive was to never acknowledge a Messiah no matter the signs because such an acknowledgment would be the death knell for their cushy set-up as the enforcers of all the Mosaic laws.

However, keeping that strategy in mind of shifting the balance of power, let's flip the theory that Jesus was a mythological figure by looking at the facts from a different perspective. Jesus was alone when he taught in the temple. He had disciples but he had no colleagues other than John the Baptist, who was also an outcast. When John the Baptist was beheaded by Herod because Herod's wife did not like that John told Herod it was not lawful for him to have married his brother's wife, Jesus found himself alone teaching John's message of repentance – a message that put him at odds with both the secular and Jewish power structure.

Matthew 4:12-17 says, "When Jesus heard that John had been arrested, he withdrew to Galilee. He left Nazareth and went to live in Capernaum by the sea, in the region of Zebulun and Naphtali, [so] that what had been said through Isaiah the prophet might be fulfilled." In the footnote of my Bible, it explains that Isaiah's prophecy of the light rising upon Zebulun and Naphtali is fulfilled in Jesus' residence at Capernaum.

This move to Capernaum marks what I believe to be the beginning of Jesus' strategy to shift the balance of power in his favor by aligning his actions to the prophesies of Isaiah in order to make it clear to any outside observers that he was the Messiah for whom they were looking.

A prophesy is a prediction. The dictionary defines it as the inspired declaration of divine will and purpose. Prophesies are usually very symbolic and open to interpretation because they arise out of the intuition and inspiration of the individual making them. The aha moment regarding their accuracy usually comes after the fact when we realize how closely the prophesy matches actual events. For instance, Nostradamus' predictions are very vague and no one really

THE MOBBING OF JESUS CHRIST 67

knows what they mean so it is very easy to match events like the collapse of the World Trade Center and the rise of the Nazi regime to them because certain phrases and language he used align with those occurrences. It is much more difficult to take one of his predictions and say exactly what will happen at some future date based on the elusive information he gives. Yet that is exactly what Jesus does with the vague prophesies of Isaiah during his final days in Jerusalem.

The very next chapter paragraph in Matthew is titled, *The Call of the First Disciples*. If we are to analyze Bible scripture with techniques such as the order in which information appears, as many Bible scholars do, then having this chapter follow the chapter in which Jesus becomes aware of John's arrest tells us that Jesus did not choose twelve disciples until after learning that his mentor (the one who baptized him) had been arrested. It was John's arrest and subsequent death that caused Jesus to implement his strategy of lining up his life to that of the mythical stories of the Messiah. These verses indicate that Jesus' designation of twelve of the many disciples he had been attracting since he was a twelve-year old child as 'the twelve' was the first step in a plan that would include an array of miracles and his own staged resurrection. As I will show, the mobbing entered into Phase 3, as described by Leymann, after one of those very public miracles was witnessed by people who brought it to the attention of Caiaphas.

Mob Strategy No. 5: Violence or threats of violence are directed against the targeted individual

In environments like the one created by the Pharisees, the truth is lethal. The truth Jesus was teaching was shining light on the doctrinal lies the Pharisees were telling the Jewish community. Like so many Christians I grew up with as a child raised in the Baptist church who attended church every Sunday, but never bothered to crack open their Bibles on their own, the Jews relied on the Pharisees for their information. They were the experts, after all, in the Mosaic Law they were imposing on the community.

Jesus was an expert too – in both the law and the truth. That gave him the advantage of being able to so eloquently and courageously point out the hypocrisy of his Pharisee colleagues. He knew how they had cherry-picked portions of their scriptures and then molded them to support the foundation for their positions of power and control over their community. It is what all power hierarchies do with information that does not comport with the world views that support their very existence and survival. They interpret or change the meaning of that information in a way that brings it in line with their world views, or in the alternative; they completely destroy the information with book burnings, manipulation of the press, tactics like shaming the people disseminating the information, propaganda and other forms of behavioral and thought modification that enhance conformance. If they are unable to get someone to conform through these various forms of pressure, they employ the kill the messenger strategy that serves to silence any voices of dissent. These are people who think they are serving the greater good of protecting their nation, family, friends and colleagues. They think they are the good guys and the voices of truth are the evil ones. They are incapable of viewing people from the point of view of human beings just like themselves. It is always good guys vs. bad guys with themselves and their world views cast as the ones on the good side.

In the eyes of the Pharisee chief priests and elders, Jesus was a lying, satanic, gluttonous, alcoholic impostor who needed to be killed. They planned for a long time how to entrap him. On several occasions, they even resorted to violence, but Jesus was able to escape harm by escaping to a nearby town or village. The verses below describe these instances of violence:

Mark 14:1-2: "Now the Passover and Unleavened Bread were two days away; <u>and the chief priests and the scribes were seeking how to seize Him by stealth and kill *Him*; for they were saying, "Not during the festival, otherwise there might be a riot of the people."</u>"

Luke 4:27-30: "And there were many lepers in Israel in the time of Elisha the prophet; and none of them was cleansed, but only Naaman the Syrian." And all *the people* in the synagogue were filled with rage as they heard these things; <u>and they got up and drove Him out of the city, and led Him to the brow of the hill on which their city had been built, in order to throw Him down the cliff. But passing through their midst, He went His way.</u>"

John 8:56-59: "Your father Abraham rejoiced to see My day, and he saw *it* and was glad." So the Jews said to Him, "You are not yet fifty years old, and have You seen Abraham?" Jesus said to them, "Truly, truly, I say to you, before Abraham was born, I am." <u>Therefore they picked up stones to throw at Him, but Jesus hid Himself and went out of the temple</u>.

As the above verses so clearly indicate, Jesus was a marked man. It was just a matter of time before the stones would hit their mark and kill him or he would not be able to escape before he was thrown off a cliff.

5

Phase III - Personnel Administration Management Gets Involved

The Ill-Thought-Out Plot of Lazarus to Give the Pharisees Their Sign

According to Leymann, the interpersonal conflicts of phases I and II of a mobbing (the original critical incident and the bullying and stigmatizing respectively) officially become a case when management steps in. From all indications, the Chief Priest Caiaphas became involved and the bullying of Jesus became a case when some Pharisees who witnessed Jesus raise Lazarus from the dead went to Caiaphas and told him that some of the Jews who saw it now believed Jesus to be the long-awaited Messiah:

> John 11:45: "Therefore, many of the Jews who came to Mary, and saw what He had done [raising Lazarus], believed in Him."

For those of you who are not familiar with the story of Lazarus, he was a man who Jesus is said to have raised from the dead. The story of Lazarus is found John 11:1-43. When the story begins, Jesus is traveling from Bethany with his disciples. He has just left the home of Lazarus and his two sisters, Martha and Mary, a few days earlier. While Jesus and his disciples are on the road, they receive word that Lazarus is ill. Jesus tells the disciples that Lazarus is sick but reassures them that Lazarus will not die from his illness. Rather, his illness will be used for the glory of God and that he, Jesus, will be glorified through it. (John 11:3-4)

Although Jesus is a positive human being, his response upon hearing that his friend is ill is a bit strange. Instead of expressing concern that his friend is ill, as one would expect from a man like Jesus, he tells them that the illness is meant to benefit him in some way and shows little concern for Lazarus' plight. He even waits two days and then tells his disciples that they are going back to Judea to awaken Lazarus. (John 11:6) The disciples interpret his use of the word 'awaken' in the spiritual way that sleep is usually used in the Bible and assure him that if Lazarus is asleep, he will be saved. Jesus corrects them and tells them that Lazarus has died an actual physical death, and they must go back to Judea, despite the fact that the last time they were there the Pharisees tried to stone him. (John 11:8-14)

While Jesus and his disciples are on the outskirts of Bethany four days after Lazarus' death, Martha meets them. She tells Jesus that if he had been there Lazarus would never have died but that since he has returned, God will give him whatever he asks for. Jesus tells Martha her brother will rise and when Martha says she knows her brother will rise in the resurrection on the last day, Jesus says to her, "I am the resurrection, and the life: he that believeth in me, though he were dead, yet shall he live." (John 11:25) After telling Jesus she believes he is the Messiah, Martha runs back to the house to get her sister Mary who is in mourning. Verse 28 says that Martha tells her sister "secretly" that Jesus has arrived, but when the Jews who are there comforting Mary see her get up abruptly and leave, they follow her out. When Jesus sees Martha and Mary approaching with the Jews following behind them, the Bible says, "He became perturbed and deeply troubled." (John 11:33)

This is the first time in the story that we see Jesus becoming perturbed and troubled. Upon hearing the news of Lazarus' illness, he waits two days before returning (verse 6) and even after Martha, a woman he loves, blames him for Lazarus' death by telling him Lazarus wouldn't have died if he had been there, Jesus still doesn't get upset. (John 11:5) Therefore, I don't think Jesus becomes perturbed and troubled over the death. I think he is perturbed and troubled that he has all these unexpected visitors. The fact that Martha secretly summons Mary indicates that Jesus did not expect anyone but the two sisters and his disciples to be at the tomb when Lazarus is raised.

As he approaches the tomb with everyone looking on, Martha reminds him that Lazarus has been in there for four days and there will likely be a horrible stench, to which Jesus reminds her that if she believes, she will see the glory of God. It is very curious that these are the same words he used with his disciples upon hearing that Lazarus was ill but that, "This illness is not to end in death, but would be for the glory of God and that the Son of God may be glorified through it." (John 11:4)

Jesus has shown no emotion whatsoever upon hearing of his friend's illness and subsequent death and for a man as empathetic as Jesus, that is absolutely unbelievable particularly since verse 5 says that Jesus loved Martha and her sister Mary and Lazarus. Instead, he says two times that it is for the glorification of God and himself. What possible glorification could Jesus find in such a tragic circumstance? Unless, as he assured his disciples upon hearing of the illness, he knew ahead of time that it would not end in death.

Now, pay attention to what Jesus says as Martha rolls the stone from the tomb:

> John 11:41-42: "So they removed the stone. Then Jesus raised His eyes, and said, "Father, I thank You that You have heard Me.[42] I knew that You always hear Me; but because of the people standing around I said it, so that they may believe that You sent Me."

This man - Jesus - who always went off alone to pray and tells us to do likewise, decides to pray out loud for the benefit of the people who have shown up unexpectedly. According to this verse, he explicitly wants them to believe that he has been sent by God as the Messiah. Then right after saying this, he cries out in a loud voice, "Lazarus, come forth," and Lazarus comes out with his grave clothes bound round his hand and foot and his face bound with a napkin. Jesus tells them to untie him and let him go. That's it. Done. No signs that he was ever dead. He comes forth from the grave as good as new after Jesus commands it. No smell, no rot, no nothing. Just a man who was dead and is now headed on his way.

The last verses in the chapter read as follows:

> Now the Passover of the Jews was near, and many went up to Jerusalem out of the country before the Passover to purify themselves. So they were seeking for Jesus, and were saying to one another as they stood in the temple, "What do you think; that He will not come to the feast at all?" Now the chief priests and the Pharisees had given orders that if anyone knew where He was, he was to report it, so that they might seize Him.

Judging from the verses above, it is clear that the raising of Lazarus from the dead happens at some time between the Passover of Jesus' second year of ministry and the final Passover when he enters Jerusalem for the last time. He has been ministering for two years and stirring up the ire of the Pharisees who were hounding and harassing him wherever he went - just waiting for him to make a slip so they could arrest him.

Lazarus and his sisters Mary and Martha were going to provide the sign that would put the harassment and all the Pharisee requests for a sign to rest and it almost worked. The problem was it worked too well and caught the attention of Caiaphas, who saw it as a sign that he needed to do something about the miracle worker who was stealing Jewish followers from him. (John 11:45, John 12:9-11)

There comes a time when we have to begin reading these stories realistically with the knowledge of science and common sense that we all possess. Jesus made it clear to his disciples that this man was not asleep - that he was physically dead. There is no room for metaphysical interpretations or metaphors whatsoever, yet that is how I have heard this story explained every time it has been preached to me. I was tempted to skip over it completely because I had no explanation for how Jesus possibly gave back life to a body that had been dead for almost a week and was beginning to rot. Then I went back to read it again from the beginning with the knowledge I had gained and write about in this book ... and the light bulb turned on.

Jesus had just left the house of Lazarus and was on the road when he received the news of Lazarus' illness. Unlike today, they did not have telephones or email to communicate with one another. It was all face-to-face back when Jesus lived. I imagine Jesus, Lazarus and his sisters did some planning while they were all together in Bethany. This family loved Jesus as much he loved them. They would have been aware of the Pharisees' harassment and vitriolic hatred for this good man they all loved. Whether it was their idea or that of Jesus, I believe someone came up with the idea for giving the Pharisees the sign they kept asking for, reasoning that it would get them off Jesus' back so that he could continue his teaching without the constant harassment and stress of getting arrested for saying the wrong thing. I believe a plan was put together whereby they would fake Lazarus' death so that Jesus could return and save him.

To their credit, their plan worked just as they planned. Verse 45 says that many of the Jews who saw it began to believe in Jesus as the Messiah. Some of the Jews even went to the Pharisees to let them know what Jesus did. Instead of getting met with amazement at this feat, however; the Pharisaic leadership viewed it as they did everything else under their prism of ego, power and prestige. They became concerned about the ripple effects of such a feat, reasoning that if some of the Jews who saw it came to believe, it wouldn't be long before others would also come to believe once word got out. They needed to get ahead of it and so they hightailed it to the chief priests and together with the Pharisees, the chief priests convened the Sanhedrin to decide what they were going to do to contain it before it got out of hand. It was at that Sanhedrin that Caiaphas decided to have Jesus killed, along with Lazarus. That way, all the main players would be properly disposed of and the story could be told in the way they wanted it told with Jesus cast as an impostor:

> John 12:10-11: "But the chief priests planned to put Lazarus to death also; because on account of him many of the Jews were going away and were believing in Jesus."

That perturbation Jesus felt on his way to Lazarus' tomb must have rippled down to the depths of his soul. The plan was on a failed track when the Jews unexpectedly showed up and Jesus made it worse by declaring for all to hear that God had sent him. I think the only witnesses he expected or wanted there were his trusted disciples and friends. I believe the assumption underlying the plan was that just having Lazarus alive after the community heard he had died would be enough to prove that Jesus was the almighty, all-powerful superman of a Messiah the Pharisees were expecting. Although it was an ill-conceived plan, Jesus wasn't trying to fool anyone but the Pharisees. He was giving them the sign they asked him for. He knew they would never change their internal paradigm of mind that would see him as the true Messiah, but I do not think that was his goal. I think, like all targeted individuals, he just wanted to be able to continue doing what he was doing without the constant harassment and threat of arrest hanging over him.

Unfortunately, it didn't turn out as I suspect Jesus intended.

As soon as Jesus gave credibility to the superhuman, all-powerful God in the sky who gave him powers to raise people from the dead, he lost control of the true message he dedicated his life to delivering after coming out of the wilderness of his ego into the enlightenment of a mind that decides never to give up truth and reality no matter the external threat to its survival. There was no putting the genie back in the bottle once the church decided to fill the New Testament with the letters of Paul whose doctrine focuses solely on the false superhuman aspect of Jesus – an aspect that never existed in truth and reality.

It all just snowballed from there and what was meant to be a single incident to solve a Pharisee harassment problem turned into a major conspiracy that negatively affected the life of not only Jesus, but Lazarus as well when he became a huge drawing card. John 12:9-10 says that Jesus was attracting large crowds who not only wanted to see him, but also Lazarus who was raised from the dead. The chief priests decided to kill Lazarus also because many Jews were believing in Jesus as the Messiah because of Lazarus. (See also John 12:17-19)

The Greater Good Rationalization Used to Justify Killing Jesus

It was not God who sent his only son to die for our sins. It was the rationalization of a cruel, manipulative, power hungry and weak man who no one had the courage to question. So, what does he do to deal with his own insecurities and vulnerability? He does the natural thing every corrupt and unaware leader of the pack at the top of the hierarchy does to any potential threat to his power base - human or otherwise. He looks for a way to eliminate the threat, but he does it under the guise that it is for everyone's good. Rationalizations come in very handy for people like Caiaphas because if they were upfront about their true motives, they would be seen for the murderers, slanderers and monsters they really are.

Caiaphas used one of the best rationalizations of all time for justifying the destruction of a person's reputation, livelihood and life in a battle to gain and retain that which cannot otherwise be gained and kept on the merits: *the greater good rationalization*:

> John 11:49-50: "But one of them, Caiaphas, who was high priest that year, said to them, "You know nothing at all nor do you take into account that it is expedient for you that one man die for the people, and that the whole nation not perish."

The *greater good* rationalization has been recycled over and over again by politicians who want to win (not earn) our vote, and we accept it every time it's used because it falls into the category of, *It is just what politicians do and there is nothing that can be done about it.* A political nominee may reason it is perfectly acceptable to assassinate his opponent's character and tell lies about his record if it makes him win the election. If you were to ask him why he does this, he would not reply by saying his motives are evil, even though they are. He would most likely justify it to you and himself on the grounds that if it makes him win office, he can accomplish a lot of good things for many people. So what if the personal reputation of his opponent is forever damaged? It is worth it, he would say, because many more people will be helped as a result.

Caiaphas used a similar argument to justify the killing of Jesus, claiming it had to be done to save the nation. The crucifixion was not the act of a loving God sending his only son to die for our sins as Christianity claims. That is a preposterous claim on its face. How does it make any sense whatsoever that the loving God of creation who breathed life into this expansive universe and everything in it would choose the destruction of a single human life as the means to save humanity? The answer is that it doesn't make any sense. It is the ideology of a limited ego consciousness imagining that God thinks like ego conscious human beings do. In our minds, the biggest sacrifice anyone can think of making is to sacrifice a child.

We would gladly give our own lives to save our child's life. Therefore, Christianity propagates the idea that since God is a loving God who gave up his only son for our sins then he must love us beyond all measure. Other than the fact that one of the Ten Commandments says, "Thou shalt not kill," and that Genesis 1:27 says we are all sons and daughters made in the image of God, it is irrational to believe that the taking of a single life saves a life, much less the lives of all humanity then and forevermore. This is false doctrine and we must begin analyzing it with a mind grounded in what we all know to be true.

The rationale we attribute to God was actually the evil and warped justification used by Caiaphas to kill one man (Jesus) in order to save the Pharisaic power structure. It was the doing of one man with the power to order the killing in the interest of national security. He convinced his colleagues and subordinates that Jesus was a threat to them because Jews were beginning to believe that Jesus was the long-awaited Messiah who would break the yoke of Roman oppression. Breaking the yoke of Roman oppression would correspondingly break the back-door deals Caiaphas made with the Roman hierarchy to give him control over his own Jewish empire.

The self-serving argument Caiaphas made that Jesus had to be killed to save the nation is the exact same argument Hitler used in claiming it was his God-given duty to kill off all Jews in order to save humanity. In Mein Kampf, Hitler wrote:

> "Should the Jew, with the aid of his Marxist creed, triumph over the people of this world, his Crown will be the funeral wreath of mankind, and this planet will once again follow its orbit through ether, without any human life on this surface, as it did millions of years ago. And so I believe today that my conduct is in accordance with the will of the Almighty Creator. In standing guard against the Jew, I am defending the handiwork of the Lord."[22]

Both Hitler and Caiaphas were deluded individuals who held power. They were the victims of their own perceptions and beliefs. They were what most people would describe as psychopathic, the dominant characteristic of which we are told is lack of conscience. Many psychologists believe the lack of conscience is what makes psychopaths impossible to treat. I think Hitler and Caiaphas would beg to differ. I think it was their belief in the righteousness of their respective causes that was guiding their decision-making. That is what makes them impossible to treat. When a person believes they are good and are resolute in their beliefs, then it is close to impossible to change their minds. The reason men like Hitler and Caiaphas are so dangerous is that they are given the reins of power whereby they have the tools at their disposal for making their subordinates conform to their beliefs. That is what authoritarianism is and it does not matter whether it is a parent in a home, a teacher in a school, a CEO in a workplace, a president of a country or a global commission; if a person is willing to abuse the power of their position to make other people conform to what they think and believe is right and good for everyone else, then we will always have incidents of individual human rights abuses.

In order to address his anxiety over Jesus' popularity and influence, Caiaphas made the criminal, immoral, cruel and calculated decision to destroy the message by destroying the messenger. It is an age-old strategy of the Bully/Bystander/Enabler/Target Model of Thought and Behavior because it is extremely effective in destroying agents of change in order to keep the status quo firmly intact.

The staged raising of Lazarus from the dead was the catalyst for the mobbing. Had it not been for Jesus' attempt to give the Pharisees the sign they kept asking for with his plan to raise Lazarus from the dead, the matter may never have come to the attention of Caiaphas. If it had not caused Caiaphas, the man at the top of the hierarchy, to become concerned about his own standing in the community; the matter would have remained a bullying problem rather than a mobbing. Once it did become a mobbing, the elimination of Jesus became the goal as it does in all cases of mobbing.

Luke 4:13 is a very interesting verse that confused me for so long until I put the puzzle pieces together and was able to come up with a coherent theory of what happened to Jesus that puts all the gospels - including some of the newly found Gospels that the Church claims are heresy - in an overall context that makes sense and aligns them with the rest of the Bible's teachings regarding ego and consciousness.

When Jesus emerges from his 40 days in the wilderness after having been tempted by the devil, Luke 4:13 says, "He [the devil] departed from him [Jesus] for a time." This verse implies that the devil, which we learn is ego in my book, *The Evolution of Good and Evil*, returns to Jesus at some point in time. I believe it returned when he learned from Nicodemus, Joseph of Arimathea or one of the other secret disciples that Caiaphas was out to kill him. The corrupt Pharisee Council forced him into adopting an ego consciousness of survival because his physical existence was at risk. No matter what he did, whether he decided to run or stay, his days were numbered once the forces of the power structure were brought to bear on him. I believe Judas was a plant [spy] the Pharisee Council used to report information back to them about what Jesus was up to. Unbeknownst to them, Jesus had spies of his own who wanted to protect him from their corrupt colleagues and boss, but who did not want to sacrifice their own positions by making their loyalty known.

Jesus had a couple of choices. He could either quit his ministry and run when he received information from his secret alliances, or he could confront his persecutors and face the consequences. When he decided he no longer wanted to run as he had done on so many previous occasions, I believe he made the conscious choice to follow the latter course of action. The knowledge his secret disciples provided to him gave Jesus an advantage over other targets who lose all control over their own destinies because they are kept ignorant of the carefully orchestrated events plotted behind closed doors, thereby rendering them powerless to do anything to change their circumstances. Given the information Jesus received, I think he was able to come up with an alternate strategy to the traditional fight or flight strategies of survival other targets must choose from.

Jesus knew what he was teaching about the nature of good and evil was the truth and if followed would turn humanity around and start it on a path toward its destiny. He knew he was the Messiah for whom they were all waiting, but the physical audience to whom he was addressing this message was expecting a different kind of savior. They were accustomed to the superhero version of God the Pharisees peddled. The Pharisees, in particular, were always asking Jesus for a sign that he was the Messiah. (Luke 11:29, Matthew 16:4, Matthew 12:39) As the Messiah and son of God, they expected Jesus to be all-powerful and all-mighty like the God they envisioned from their literal interpretation of the scriptures. After one of their many requests for a sign, the Bible says Jesus sighed from the depth of his spirit and said, "Why doth this generation seek after a sign? verily I say unto you, There shall no sign be given unto this generation." He then got in a boat and headed off to the other shore. (Mark 8:11-13)

Anyone who reads the New Testament account of Jesus cannot help but feel his frustration at trying to explain God to people who had preconceived notions. They refused to consider any reality other than the one they held in their own minds about God. It does no good for a person to study facts and debate issues with lazy minds that accept what they're told because it benefits their cause or fits their world view. They do not want to put the same effort into determining truth because it would destroy what they have a stake in believing on face value. When circumstances got to a tipping point, I think Jesus decided that if you can't beat them then join them and he incorporated their requests for a sign into a strategy for making his immanent execution mirror the prophesies of Isaiah in the Old Testament.

The New Testament Gospels of Jesus do not provide a time line of events so we can never know exactly when Jesus began planning how to align events in his own life to those that the prophet Isaiah predicted regarding the Messiah, but we do know that Jesus's own words indicate a purposeful attempt to plant the seeds in the minds of his followers that he was the savior Isaiah predicted would come. In Matthew 12:38-40, when the Pharisees again ask for a sign from him, he doesn't sigh as he did before and tell them there will be no sign. Instead, Jesus seems rather defiant when he tells them, "An evil and adulterous generation craves for a sign; and yet no sign will be given to it but the sign of Jonah the prophet; for just as Jonah was three days and three nights in the belly of the sea monster, so will the Son of Man [a term Jesus always used to refer to himself] be three days and three nights in the heart of the earth." This is the first reference Jesus makes to his crucifixion, burial and resurrection. This exchange is repeated in Matthew 16:1, after which Jesus leaves and warns his disciples to beware of the teachings of the Pharisees and Sadducees.

The Bible passage immediately following this statement says that Jesus asked his disciples, "Who do people say that the Son of Man is?" (Matthew 16:13) It is curious to me that Jesus would be interested in finding out what people say he is. Why would a Messiah who was sent from up above by God to save future generations from sin be concerned about what people think of him? It seems like a rather mundane concern voiced by an egotistical human being who is concerned with his own self-image and not that of a divine godhead whose sole mission for being on this earth in human form is to save

THE MOBBING OF JESUS CHRIST   83

us from sin. Again, I don't know how this was supposed to work and I have never heard any preacher explain how Jesus had this communicated to him beforehand other than he was God in human form on earth. And if that is the case, why does Jesus say the kingdom of God is within all of us? Why did God need a middleman separate from us to give us access to something that is integral to being human? What was the point for having a human being physically sacrificed for mankind's salvation when the Bible makes it clear from Genesis on that all human beings are made in the image of God?

None of it makes logical sense until it is viewed from the perspective of Jesus as a target of a gang of powerful thugs determined to see him dead. Jesus knew it was just a matter of time before the chief priests would have something to hang their hats on for an arrest. Once Jesus was in custody, they could rig the trial in their favor [as they did] to get him crucified.

I do not think Jesus was concerned with the image people had of him because of any egotistical concerns over what people thought of him. I believe it was because he needed to get a handle on the entire situation, including people's perception of him, for his strategy to be successful. If his plan to get the Pharisees to believe he was the Messiah was going to work, he needed to have some knowledge about what they expected to see in a Messiah. His disciples tell him that some people think he is Elijah and others believe he is John the Baptist or Jeremiah. Those answers indicate a population that views Jesus as just another prophet. Then Jesus asks the disciples who they think he is and Simon Peter tells him that he is the Messiah, the Son of the living God. That's the answer Jesus needs to hear and he tells Peter that flesh and blood did not reveal this truth to him. It could only have come to him by way of the "heavenly Father." Peter's answer gives Jesus the comfort level that the time is right for the twelve disciples to carry on his work.

Jesus then orders the twelve to tell no one that he is the Messiah and from that time on, he begins to tell them how he must go to Jerusalem and suffer greatly from the elders, the chief priests and the scribes; but that on the third day he will be raised. (Matthew 16:20-21) Jesus had by that time formulated an exit strategy and he needed his disciples to stay quiet until it came to fruition. After his conversation with them, and particularly based upon the answer Peter gave him, I believe Jesus was confident they understood what he taught them and that due to the number of them, they would be able to spread the true message of salvation and repentance much further than either he or John the Baptist before him were able to do alone. Jesus repeats his statement about being killed and raised on the third day in Matthew 17:22 when they are all in Galilee and then again in Matthew 20:17-19, while they are all on their way to Jerusalem for their final Passover together. (See also Mark 8:31, Mark 9:30-31, Mark 10:32-34, Luke 9:22 and Luke 9:44).

6
Phase IV: Incorrect Diagnoses
The Tables Get Turned

L eymann says Phase IV of a mobbing is when incorrect diagnoses (assessments) are made of the targeted individual. In my opinion, there are two parts to this phase: (1) incorrect diagnoses made by people who have no knowledge that a mobbing is taking place, but who nonetheless observe behavior in the targeted individual that is outside the norm, and (2) incorrect diagnoses made by the perpetrators of the mobbing with a purposeful and malicious intent to harm the targeted individual.

An example of the first one could be when Jesus is talking with the crowds and he blurts out, 'Why are you trying to kill me?" They tell him that he is crazy and ask him who is trying to kill him? (See John 7:17-21) However, on second thought, depending upon who was in the crowd, it could also be an example of the second one because people who are capable of bullying and mobbing behavior will always deny they are doing what they are actually doing.

At the time Jesus says this, he has probably heard from Nicodemus, Joseph of Arimathea or some other of his secret disciples that the Council wants him dead. To the naive masses, it would be inconceivable that their religious leaders could commit such an act against an innocent and good man. After all, the members of the Council were considered pillars of the community who proudly displayed their tassels wherever they went. How could such men plot to kill someone like Jesus? It is impossible in the minds of normal people that someone would be killed simply for who they are and so they reflexively call Jesus crazy instead of looking at the Council members as crazy. It is the same reflex reaction of people who refuse to believe that a clean-cut college student could also be a rapist or that the charming lawyer next door could be abusing his/her spouse.

When Leif, the factory worker, began displaying anger and frustration over his treatment and the wrong instructions he was being given, his co-workers automatically tagged him as a volatile and incompetent employee, even though he had previously proved his competence at his job. This knee jerk tendency of others to easily view targeted individuals as something they had never been before works to the advantage of the perpetrators of the mobbing. The perpetrators of the mobbing know that if the targeted employee seeks the help of a mental health professional, it does little good because most psychologists/psychiatrists know nothing about the mobbing phenomenon and will likely misdiagnose the targeted individual. He/she will then get labeled with an incorrect diagnosis such as "paranoia, "querulous paranoia, "manic-depressive illness, "adjustment disorder or "character disorder;" thereby severely limiting the targeted individual's chances of returning to the labor market in a comparable position with comparable pay.[18]

Below are some other verses where Jesus is accused of being crazy and/or possessed:

> Mark 3:20-22: "And He came home, and the crowd gathered again, to such an extent that they could not even eat a meal. When His own people heard *of this*, they went out to take custody of Him; for they were saying, "He has lost His senses." The scribes who came down from Jerusalem were saying, "He is possessed by Beelzebul," and "He casts out the demons by the ruler of

the demons."

John 8:48-52: "The Jews answered and said to Him, "Do we not say rightly that You are a Samaritan and have a demon?" [49] Jesus answered, "I do not have a demon; but I honor My Father, and you dishonor Me. But I do not seek My glory; there is One who seeks and judges. Truly, truly, I say to you, if anyone keeps My word he will never see death." The Jews said to Him, "Now we know that You have a demon. Abraham died, and the prophets *also*; and You say, 'If anyone keeps My word, he will never taste of death.'"

It wasn't just the crowds and Pharisees who were calling him crazy; even his own family did. (Mark 3:20). That is not atypical in these situations. Targeted individuals can become obsessed with what is happening to them. When they come home each day telling their family members what is going on at work, their family members have as much trouble believing them as the crowds did believing Jesus. This unbelief is understandable given that most people look at human behavior through a lens of rationality. Since the mob purposely destroys rationality with its lies and other strategies in order to rid the targeted individual from their midst, the stories being told by the targeted individual sound exaggerated and untrue. Phrases like, "you must be imagining that" or "people are not that cruel" are what targeted individuals must endure hearing from the people closest to them. When their own family doesn't believe them or thinks they are exaggerating, then targets begin doubting themselves. Once doubt sets in, all is lost. The paranoia, anxiety and depression become all too real and give credence to the false diagnoses people are making about them.

Unfortunately, these kinds of phrases are not only uttered by family members. They are told to us by well-meaning friends and colleagues who would rather not make it part of their world view that human beings just like them are capable of such deceitful, manipulative and depraved behavior. One Jewish holocaust survivor I read about recounted how people would tell her she should put the whole experience behind her after having suffered so much. However, the reaction that caused her to quit talking about it completely was when she was told, "You must be exaggerating. Human beings don't do things like that to other human beings."[19]

We hear all about the holocaust and the six million Jews who were killed, but something we do not hear so much about is the great number of Jewish survivors who suffered from Post-Traumatic Stress Syndrome (PTSD) in the subsequent years because of the trauma they endured.[20] Below is a concise description of the factors that contribute to PTSD:

> "Complex prolonged period of negative stress in which certain factors are present, which may include any of captivity, lack of means of escape, entrapment, repeated violation of confusion, and - crucially - lack of control, loss of control and disempowerment. It is the overwhelming nature of the events and the inability (helplessness, lack of knowledge, lack of support etc.) of the person trying to deal with those events that leads to the development of Complex PTSD. Situations which might give rise to Complex PTSD include bullying, harassment, abuse, domestic violence, stalking, long-term caring for a disabled relative, unresolved grief, exam stress over a period of years, mounting debt, contact experience, PTSD can potentially arise from any boundaries, betrayal, rejection, bewilderment, etc."[21]

In my opinion, Jesus also may have suffered from PTSD. One of the common symptoms of PTSD is sudden angry or violent outbursts.[22] Jesus, as a sufferer of PTSD, could explain his outburst in the temple where he threw the money changers out, as well as the incident where he lost many disciples because he told them to drink his blood and eat his flesh. (See John 6:51-66) Even his plan to raise Lazarus from the grave. These were all ill-thought-out actions and words by a man who was so logical, even-tempered and a master at choosing his words wisely. Luke 19:45-48 describes the scene with the money changers as follows:

> "Jesus entered the temple and began to drive out those who were selling, saying to them, "It is written, 'And My house shall be a house of prayer,' but you have made it a robbers' den." And He was teaching daily in the temple; but the chief priests and the scribes and the leading men among the people were trying to destroy Him, and they could not find anything that they might do, for all the people were hanging on to every word He said."

Even Jesus' impassioned condemnation of the Pharisees in Matthew 23 that I cited earlier in the book where he repeatedly calls them hypocrites, blind fools, snakes, vipers and whitewashed tombs was so out of character for him and could have been an emotional outburst that is symptomatic of people suffering from PTSD. Professor Westhues writes, "As the attacks continue day in and day out the target begins to be worn down and eventually will make a mistake. Perhaps they will have an emotional outburst and lash back at the bully. This is stereotypical in mobbing cases and this incident will be used to turn the tables on the target as the bully will loudly proclaim that this proves that the target is the real troublemaker. This often gives management, who has done nothing about the bullying, the opportunity to bring formal disciplinary measures against the target and the victim winds up being the one who is punished."[23]

It is telling that Jesus ends his diatribe against the Pharisees in Matthew 23 by saying, "You testify against yourselves that you are the descendants of those who murdered the prophets. Go ahead, then, and complete what your ancestors started!" This statement of his shows that Jesus knew they were out to murder him. It is hard to imagine the mix of emotions he must have been feeling when he uttered words that were so uncharacteristic of him, but I can most assuredly say that anger was in the mix – the righteous anger of a man who was being so unfairly treated for having done nothing to justify such treatment.

After being accused of mental instability and/or insanity in Phase 4 of a mobbing, with Phase 5 clearly becoming an inevitability, the human mind begins to break down with the knowledge that there is absolutely nothing that can be done to stop the force of the mob from trampling the targeted individual to the ground and, in the case of Jesus, killing him. So what does a target do? What can a target do under such circumstances to not only save himself, but also save the work, reputation and accomplishments he has spent a lifetime building? The answer is nothing. There is nothing any target can do to save the life he/she has built up to that point because the whole goal of the mob is to destroy that work, life and reputation. And when the man at the top of the hierarchy is leading the mob's actions, as Caiaphas was, achieving the goal of destruction becomes an absolute certainty.

Although the Lazarus incident gave Caiaphas the justification for going after Jesus, it was not an offense for which Jesus could be arrested. His outburst in the temple, albeit atypical of Jesus, is quite typical in instances of mobbing. It was, in fact, the incident that Westhues talks about that allows the tables to be turned on a targeted individual. In the case of Jesus, the temple outburst gave Caiaphas the ammunition he needed. A charge like destruction of temple property would have gotten Jesus arrested on legitimate grounds. Once in custody, Caiaphas could get his ducks in a row to build a case for execution against Jesus, which is exactly what he did with all the false witnesses and evidence he gathered and used at the mock trial.

7
Phase V: Expulsion
Mission Accomplished

In his meeting with the Sanhedrin when Caiaphas made it clear to all the Pharisees in attendance that Jesus needed to be eliminated, their goal became Jesus' arrest. By the time Jesus entered Jerusalem for the final Passover, Caiaphas and the chief priests had their plan put together and were ready to execute it:

> Matthew 26:3-5: "Then the chief priests and the elders of the people assembled in the palace of the high priest, who was called Caiaphas, and they consulted together to arrest Jesus by treachery and put him to death. But they said, "Not during the festival, that there may not be a riot among the people."

Unbeknownst to them, Jesus had a plan of his own which he had begun carrying out by aligning the prophesies of Isaiah with his planned murder. Jesus's own words indicate a purposeful attempt to plant the seeds that he was the savior Isaiah predicted would come.

Jesus predicts his death in Matthew 16:21-23 and then repeats the prediction two more times in Matthew 17:22-23 and Matthew 20:27-29. Likewise, the Gospels of Mark and Luke also contain three paragraphs titled the first, second and third prediction of the passion. In Matthew, the predictions read as follows:

1. Jesus Predicts His Death: "From that time on, Jesus began to show his disciples that he must go to

Jerusalem and suffer greatly from the elders, the chief priests, and the scribes, and be killed and on the third day be raised." (Matthew 16:21)

2. Jesus Predicts His Death a Second Time: "As they were gathering in Galilee, Jesus said to them, "The Son of Man is to be handed over to men, and they will kill him, and he will be raised on the third day." And they were overwhelmed with grief." (Matthew 17:22-23)

3. Jesus Predicts His Death a Third Time: "As Jesus was going up to Jerusalem, he took the twelve [disciples] aside by themselves, and said to them on the way, "Behold, we are going up to Jerusalem, and the Son of Man will be handed over to the chief priests and the scribes, and they will condemn him to death." (Matthew 20:17- 18)

Jesus tells his disciples on three separate occasions that he is going to die and be raised on the third day. Repeating something you want someone to remember is not how myths are created, but it is exactly how someone might go about getting a person to place some significance on a future event that will be occurring. In this instance, Jesus wants his disciples to know he will be killed but not to worry; he will be raised from the dead on the third day; just like Horus and the other mythological gods.

In the second and third predictions, Jesus says he will be delivered over to the chief priests and the teachers of the law, and they will condemn him to death. As I have shown, Jesus knew the Council planned to kill him, but I believe the day and time of his arrest was orchestrated by Jesus himself. The proof of this is at the Last Supper when he identifies Judas as the traitor and then tells him to go and do what he must do. (Matthew 26:20-25, Mark 14:17-23, Luke 22:21-23 and John 13:21-30). How do we rationally explain that Jesus knew it was Judas who was going to betray him? The only way I can think of that Jesus knew Judas was his betrayer is because he heard it from one or more of his secret disciples.

Later in the evening, when Judas is accompanied by a crowd brandishing swords and clubs, along with the chief priests and elders who have come to arrest him, Jesus tells Judas to do what he came to do. When one of Jesus' followers draws his sword, he admonishes him saying once again that this is the way the scriptures must be fulfilled.

> Matthew 26:51-54: "And behold, one of those who were with Jesus reached and drew out his sword, and struck the slave of the high priest and cut off his ear. Then Jesus said to him, "Put your sword back into its place; for all those who take up the sword shall perish by the sword. Or do you think that I cannot appeal to My Father, and He will at once put at My disposal more than twelve legions of angels? How then will the Scriptures be fulfilled, *which say that it must happen this way?*"

Some modern-day interpretations of the Gospel of Judas indicate that Judas might have been working with Jesus to arrange his capture. I doubt this interpretation based on the actions of Judas himself. According to Matthew 27:3-5, Judas returned the money given to him by the chief priests out of guilt, telling them he betrayed Jesus. Matthew 27:3-5 describes the scene between Judas and the chief priests and elders as follows:

> "Then when Judas, who had betrayed Him, saw that He had been condemned, he felt remorse and returned the thirty pieces of silver to the chief priests and elders, saying, "I have sinned by betraying innocent blood." But they said, "What is that to us? See to that yourself!" And he threw the pieces of silver into the temple sanctuary and departed; and he went away and hanged himself."

There would have been no guilt if Judas was working with Jesus; nor would he have committed suicide as he did. Also, with Jesus being the man he was, he would never have called Judas out as his betrayer so publicly at the Last Supper if Judas was in fact trying to help him. I explain Judas' motivation for betraying Jesus in detail in my book, *Morality Within the Framework of Reality*, but basically, I think it is far more likely that Judas was a paid informant who was a victim of the 'need to know' strategy of the hierarchy. I don't think he ever imagined that the plan was to execute Jesus when he agreed to spy for the chief priests and elders. When he found out, that is when he went to the priests to make them change their minds and was told to look to himself for his own role in the matter. When he did look to himself, he was racked with guilt for his role in sending such a good man to what he believed was his death.

Jesus knew in the Garden of Gethsemane that Judas was coming back with the soldiers to arrest him, and I believe he was experiencing sensory overload where he "was in such agony and he prayed so fervently that his sweat became like drops of blood falling on the ground." (Luke 22:44) Hopelessness and despair entered Jesus' core consciousness in the Garden. He was frantic and his thinking was distorted. Jesus knew that the final part of the plan he put together was about to be executed and he was having serious doubts about it. Mark 14:32-42 describes the scene as follows:

> 14:32 They came to a place named Gethsemane; and He said to His disciples, "Sit here until I have prayed."

> 14:33 And He took with Him Peter and James and John, and <u>began to be very distressed and troubled.</u>

> 14:34 And He said to them, "My soul is deeply grieved to the point of death; remain here and keep watch."

> 14:35 And He went a little beyond them and fell to the ground and began to pray that if it were possible, the hour might pass Him by.

> 14:36 And He was saying, "Abba! Father! All things are possible

for You; remove this cup from Me; yet not what I will, but what You will."

14:37 And He came and found them sleeping, and said to Peter, "Simon, are you asleep? Could you not keep watch for one hour?

14:38 Keep watching and praying that you may not come into temptation; the spirit is willing, but the flesh is weak."

14:39 Again He went away and prayed, saying the same words.

14:40 And again He came and found them sleeping, for their eyes were very heavy; and they did not know what to answer Him.

14:41 And He came the third time, and said to them, "Are you still sleeping and resting? It is enough; the hour has come; behold, the Son of Man is being betrayed into the hands of sinners.

14:42 Get up, let us be going; behold, the one who betrays Me is at hand!

In verse 14:41 above, Jesus does not say the Son of Man is given up into the hands of God. He says the Son of Man is being betrayed into the hands of sinners. There was nothing righteous or good about what happened to Jesus. He was trapped, as all targets of mobbing become trapped. Jesus really needed support, but his disciples were in the dark about his plan. They did not know what to do or say to help him. Since there was no one around he could talk to about his distress, he should have listened to his own heart. When a decision causes us as much anguish and pain in our own minds as Jesus was experiencing in Gethsemane, we should always take a step back and think on it some more.

Jesus prayed, "Abba, Father, all things are possible unto thee;

take away this cup from me; nevertheless, not what I will, but what thou wilt." I believe God was speaking to Jesus in undeniable terms. Jesus was praying "not my will, but thine [God's], be done;" yet he was experiencing such unbelievable pain and mental anguish at this request. For a man like Jesus, this mental chaos should have been the sign he was looking for to let him know that what he was about to do was not God's will. Mental chaos is always a sign that we are headed in a wrong direction. Although I believe Jesus had very few options, he still had them. He could have gathered up his disciples and gone off to a different town as he had done several times before. It would have given him an opportunity to calm his mind and reassess his plan to see if some of the assumptions upon which it was based were false. If he had done so, I believe he would have discovered that his plan violated his two greatest commandments because it was not based on truth. That must be the foundation for all decision-making or else we risk hurting ourselves and/or others.

Jesus should have listened to his gut and left the Garden before the soldiers arrived with Judas because even though he anticipated the torture and pain of the crucifixion, he could never have anticipated the vitriolic hatred he received from the religious men he knew so well; as well as the mob of people they turned against him. (Matthew 27:20, Mark 15:11) In the upside-down world created by corrupted human minds, this good man with the pure consciousness of God was treated like something less than an animal deserving to be kicked, whipped, slapped, maligned and spat upon.

It was the same dynamic at work in Hitler-led Germany. So many times, throughout the Nuremberg trials, the transcripts show how the Jews were referred to as sub-human. They were put at the level of cockroaches in Nazi Germany. They begged their persecutors for mercy. However, one doesn't grant mercy to or protect and nourish the consciousness of cockroaches - one exterminates the pesky little rodents.

This reprogramming of the human mind had to be done so that individuals like Mengele would not feel guilty about the morally reprehensible acts they were committing. Those same acts are considered repugnant and wrong to a rational mind that values human life. By getting the population to adopt the belief that Jews were sub-human, as Goebbels and his propaganda ministers constantly referred to them, they were relieved of responsibility and accountability for the killing of their fellow human beings. This process of reprogramming and mind manipulation must be done by power abusers to the enablers and bystanders of the world in order to get their buy-in of the agenda, whatever it may be.

Jesus' story is a solid case study in how mind manipulation, propaganda and all the underhanded tactics used in mobbing work. We should have begun studying him and his life with that lens 2,000 plus years ago to prevent mobbing and cancellation from ever happening again. At the very least, or most for that matter, it could have helped to prevent the holocaust and all the other ethnic cleansings that have taken place since.

8
The Groupthink of the Mob

The Mock Trial of Jesus

To really understand how mobbing works, one must understand how the herd mentality of the animal kingdom works. The herd acts as a whole - a one. There is no room for individual thought or action. Anything that affects the herd affects the one [individual] not the other way around. In the case of a mobbing, the targeted individual has been labeled a troublemaker and thereby a threat to the herd. The strategies of mobbing are thereby used to place the targeted individual outside the herd for purposes of destruction. The odds for survival are zero if one tries to use the tools of logic and truth to combat the herd's aggression because the herd has already collectively decided the righteousness of its course of action.

Herd mentality is at the core of what has come to be known as groupthink. Not coincidentally, groupthink is at the heart of bullying and mobbing behaviors. In cases where the group is headed by a dictatorial authoritarian situated at the top of the hierarchy who has no qualms about killing the opposition, as was the case with Caiaphas, I would go so far as to say that groupthink is inherent in the process. In such situations, the group can easily become a mindless group of automatons who follow the leader no matter where he leads them.

Irving Lester Janis was the research psychologist at Yale University and a professor emeritus at the University of California,

Berkeley, who coined the term *groupthink*. Janis described groupthink as the process of collective decision-making that results in errors which are sometimes critical, because the one key factor in making decisions becomes consensus.

In the case of Jesus, the critical error caused by groupthink was his execution. Unfortunately, he was just one of many innocent people who have been convicted for crimes they did not commit because of the critical errors of the groupthink dynamic. Irving identified eight symptoms of groupthink as follows:[25]

1. Sense of invulnerability that encourage excessive optimism and risk-taking.

2. Discrediting of warnings that may challenge the group's assumptions.

3. Unquestioned belief in the morality of the group.

4. Negative stereotyping of rivals outside the group.

5. Direct pressure is applied to any 'disloyal' member of the group who questions the group's stereotypes and assumptions viewing such opposition as disloyalty.

6. Self-Censorship of ideas that differ from the group consensus.

7. Illusion of unanimity created among group members where silence is viewed as consent.

8. Existence of mind guards who shield the group from dissenting information.

Jesus's mock trial is an example of groupthink at its finest. Most of the symptoms of groupthink listed above can be identified as one goes through the trial transcript line-by-line; and all the symptoms can be identified from the Gospels of Matthew, Mark, Luke and John as they detail Jesus's ordeal with the Pharisees.

Below is the account of the trial taken from Mark 14:53-65.

The Mock Trial of Jesus in Mark 14:53-65

14:53 They led Jesus away to the high priest; and all the chief priests and the elders and the scribes gathered together.

14:54 Peter had followed Him at a distance, right into the courtyard of the high priest; and he was sitting with the officers and warming himself at the fire.

14:55 Now the chief priests and the whole Council kept trying to obtain testimony against Jesus to put Him to death, and they were not finding any.

14:56 For many were giving false testimony against Him, but their testimony was not consistent.

14:57 Some stood up and began to give false testimony against Him, saying,

14:58 "We heard Him say, 'I will destroy this temple made with hands, and in three days I will build another made without hands.'"

14:59 Not even in this respect was their testimony consistent.

14:60 The high priest stood up and came forward and questioned Jesus, saying, "Do You not answer? What is it that these men are testifying against You?"

14:61 But He kept silent and did not answer. Again the high priest was questioning Him, and saying to Him, "Are You the Christ, the Son of the Blessed One?"

14:62 And Jesus said, "I am; and you shall see the Son of Man sitting at the right hand of Power, and coming with the clouds of heaven."

14:63 Tearing his clothes, the high priest said, "What further need do we have of witnesses?

14:64 You have heard the blasphemy; how does it seem to you?" And they all condemned Him to be deserving of death.

14:65 Some began to spit at Him, and to blindfold Him, and to beat Him with their fists, and to say to Him, "Prophesy!" And the officers received Him with slaps in the face.

Mark 14:55 makes clear that the goal of the chief priests at the trial was to put Jesus to death. There was no presumption of innocence in Caiaphas' courtroom and truth had no place when the arbiters of truth were "looking for evidence against Jesus so that they could put him to death, but they did not find any." [verse 55]

It is interesting to note that there were elders and teachers of the law [lawyers] in attendance and not a one of them spoke up and said that their inability to find any evidence against Jesus may have been an indication that he was innocent. These teachers of the law and elders, all of whom were members of the Council, knew it was Caiaphas' desire to kill Jesus; yet not a one of them voiced any concern about how this stated goal was not only immoral and unethical, it was also against the very laws they were tasked with upholding. Caiaphas set out to convict an innocent man of an executable offense and all of them were on board with committing the injustice.

Since the facts proved innocence, they had to come up with their own set of facts to prove guilt. Verse 55 says they searched for false evidence against Jesus but were unable to find any; so then they turned to snitches and other undesirable people who were willing to lie for them. However, even in that endeavor, they were unable to get the stories of their false witnesses to line up. (Verse 56)

Caiaphas' failure to find false evidence and believable liars who could get their stories straight put the desperate and maniacal high priest in a difficult spot and his desperation is obvious when he jumps on Jesus' foreshadowing of his inevitable death as a justification to kill him. (Verses 60-63) When Caiaphas asks Jesus if he is the Son of God,

Jesus specifically refers to himself as the Son of Man. However, even an honest answer which exculpates the man does not stop a vengeful power abuser like Caiaphas. He does not stop until he gets the answer he needs, even if that answer must be made up by his own sick and maniacal mind which is desperate to get this innocent man executed.

The external, physical façade the Pharisee Council was operating in may have been labeled a Hall of Justice but that did nothing to change the internal, unjust motive of the men comprising the Council to convict a man they all knew was innocent of the crimes of which he was accused. When Caiaphas found that the physical façade of the process of justice was failing him, he turned to what he knew would work given the character of all the men situated below him in the hierarchy. He knew the weak-kneed, greedy, hypocritical vipers and snakes would follow his lead as they had done every time before. He knew the teachers of the law who twisted the law so many times before to silence the voices of dissent would not suddenly decide to do their duty under the law and tell him what a mockery he was making of the trial.

Caiaphas' charge of blasphemy was a lie and everyone in the room knew it, but that fact got lost behind all the blustering, tearing of robes, spitting and slapping going on. All Caiaphas needed to do is yell with outrage, "He has blasphemed" and all his little minions standing around so ready to please him jumped right on the bandwagon and began abusing Jesus to show their loyalty. It is the same disgusting display of cowardice and conformity Hitler could always depend on from his minions and it is what many CEOs and vice presidents rely on to keep the voices of creativity and change within their organizations silent, knowing that change will send them into unfamiliar territory for which their lack of integrity and knowledge will be ill-equipped to handle.

I recently read a wonderful illustration of how some politicians use the same kind of blustering to quell two-way debate in forums supposedly set up for debate. The particular politician involved was the head of a congressional committee discussing immigration. He opened the hearing by warning his colleagues not to use the term *illegal immigrant* during their discussions by explaining, "Our citizens are not — the people in this country are not illegal. They are out of status. They are new Americans that are immigrants." He actually uttered this sentence with a straight face. He believes we are idiots, but do not for one second think he is one. We have made that fatal mistake for far too long. Most people no longer vote because they have become resigned to these kinds of shenanigans played by the corrupt power players who run our nation. Last time I checked, I think the House of Representatives had an approval rating in the single digits and the Senate wasn't much better. What we have failed to comprehend is that word games like these are the hallmark of evil because they are attempts to hide the truth. This man's opening statement warning the delegates not to use the proper word in the debate they were about to have indicates he had no interest in having an honest discussion on the issue of immigration. He would rather redefine the debate so that only one side of the issue is considered. What the heck is an "out of status, new American who is an immigrant" anyway? What does that mean? It is just a jumble of words that makes absolutely no sense - and that is the intent. He wants to jumble and confuse our minds while he frames the debate in his favor. Corruption, which is endemic in politics, takes place in this kind of theater of the absurd. This is the arena where bullies and the mob always operate. By vaguely threatening the members of the committee to believe the fantasy of a jumbled group of words that make no sense, he can confuse them (and us) long enough to rig the game in his favor and get the outcome he desires. Since he's the man in charge, who among his colleagues is going to risk getting marginalized to point out his absurdity? If they do not want to rock the boat and risk getting labeled a troublemaker and non-team player, they will consent to this altered reality and make their judgments accordingly.

This is how evil operates and it's time to wake up to it. Honest people have no need to make up words that make no sense. Truth is good enough for them and they have the character to insist on making truth the foundation for problem solving in all arenas, even if the outcome does not serve their own interests but solves the problem.

Caiaphas was faced with the same dilemma as this politician. The truth would not get him the outcome he wanted. Under Roman law, blasphemy (even a false conviction of blasphemy) was not an executable offense. Caiaphas and the other chief priests would have to come up with more substantial lies about Jesus in order to bring him before Pilate with charges that were executable under Roman law.

Jesus before Pilate

Although Caiaphas was successful in getting the Council to convict Jesus, he had one more hurdle to overcome before his goal of total elimination was achieved. Under Roman law, blasphemy (even a false conviction of blasphemy) was not an executable offense. (John 18:30-31) Even though Caiaphas got the Council to convict Jesus, he had to lie to Pilate to achieve his goal of killing him.

> "The Jews say to Pilate, Our law commands us not to put any one to death. We desire that he may be crucified, because he deserves the death of the cross."[26]

The cowards needed Pilate to do their dirty work. Caiaphas and the chief priests brought Jesus to Pilate under the three false accusations listed below (See Luke 23:2-5):

(1) Jesus opposed the payment of taxes to Caesar.
(2) Jesus was inciting the people.
(3) Jesus claimed to be a king.

All three accusations above were out and out lies. Jesus specifically told the people to pay to Caesar what was Caesar's; (Mark 12:13-17) when Peter began to fight the soldiers who came to arrest him, Jesus told him those who live by the sword die by the sword; (Matthew 26:52) and Jesus went to a mountain to pray when the people wanted to make him king. (John 6:15) Even still, Caiaphas knew he was in the position to tell all these lies about Jesus without consequence because he was part of a corrupt power structure that makes and breaks the rules at their convenience. When the truth is in their favor, they will tell it and when it threatens them, they will lie without batting an eye. There was nothing Jesus could say in his defense to Pilate because it was his word against Caiaphas. Jesus had no witnesses, followers, disciples or friends willing to testify on his behalf. They had all been scared off by Caiaphas and the temple priests.

When Pilate questions Jesus, he finds him guilty of nothing. (Matthew 27:23, Mark 15:14, Luke 23:14). However, the chief priests and scribes had come this far with all their harassment, lies, abuse and mockery of justice. They were not about to let Pilate release Jesus, and they used all the power of their positions to demand the crucifixion of Jesus:

> Luke 23:18-25: But they cried out all together, saying, "Away with this man, and release for us Barabbas!" (He was one who had been thrown into prison for an insurrection made in the city, and for murder.) Pilate, wanting to release Jesus, addressed them again, but they kept on calling out, saying, "Crucify, crucify Him!" And he said to them the third time, "Why, what evil has this man done? I have found in Him no guilt *demanding* death; therefore I will punish Him and release Him." But they were insistent, with loud voices asking that He be crucified. And their voices *began* to prevail. And Pilate pronounced sentence that their demand be granted. And he released the man they were asking for who had been

thrown into prison for insurrection and murder, but he delivered Jesus to their will.

Pilate knew the low character of the men with whom he was dealing. He knew perfectly well it was out of their own self-interests (envy) that the chief priests handed Jesus over to him and he wanted no part in sending an innocent man to his death. (Matthew 27:18, Mark 15:10) Even though Pilate tried unsuccessfully to get Jesus released, it does not in any way change the fact that his final decision to cave in to pressure for fear of a riot breaking out was a cowardly one. (Luke 23:6-12)

What price is a human life? By washing his hands of the whole mess, Pilate took the easy way out. If he had stopped to think or cared enough about the fact that he was sending an innocent man to an agonizing crucifixion, he might have been able to resolve the situation without a riot breaking out. He could have released Barabbas and held Jesus in custody on another charge until the crowd cooled down. He could have met with Caiaphas and the priests directly and negotiated with them; or he could even have sent Jesus to another court for trial. There were any number of avenues Pilate could have pursued to help Jesus. The reason he didn't is because his own self-interests were at stake.

The repercussions of Pilate's failure to act have reverberated down through history. Josef Goebbels, Hitler's propaganda minister, loved using passion plays showing the Jews yelling for Jesus to be crucified. These plays were very effective in promoting the anti-semitic sentiment required for the effective implementation of the final solution. The verses regarding how the chief priests stirred up the crowds are conveniently not mentioned. (Mark 15:6-15, Matthew 27:20) Also not mentioned is Chapter IV, verses 16-21 in *The Gospel of Nicodemus, Formerly Called the Acts of Pontius Pilate*, where it says many of the Jews were in tears because they did not want Jesus to die:

"But when the governor looked upon the people that were present and the Jews, he saw many of the Jews in tears, and said to the chief priests of the Jews, All the people do not desire his death. The elders of the Jews answered to Pilate, We and all the people came hither for this very purpose, that he should die. Pilate saith to them, Why should he die? They said to him, Because he declares himself to be the Son."[27]

As the Jews were crying over Jesus, the chief priests were continuing to call for his death and outrageously saying that the Jews who were there in tears were the ones who wanted it. To me, this passage conclusively proves that the crowd was not there voluntarily. They were pressured to be there by the chief priests who needed them there to make their case that everyone, not just Caiaphas, wanted Jesus to die.

We simply do not understand the power of authority figures in all areas of our society to manipulate the minds of the people they control, whether it be in a home, a classroom, a workplace or a country. The people in the crowd would not have chosen Barabbas if their leaders - the ones with authority over them - had not pressured them to do so. We really must reassess our illogical views on authority and our tendency to marginalize people who question authority. Authority, in and of itself, is not a good quality deserving of respect. Hitler was a prime example of that misconception, which is why he loved the concept of authority and the hierarchical structures that institutionalize it.

However, as successful as the chief priests were in intimidating the crowds to yell for the release of Barabbas over Jesus; what is even more incredible to me is that the two criminals who were crucified beside Jesus felt compelled to heap insults on him when they witnessed the chief priests, scribes and elders making fun of Jesus while he was helpless on the cross and in no position to answer back:

Mark 15:27-32: "Those passing by were hurling abuse at Him, wagging their heads, and saying, "Ha! You who are going to destroy the temple and rebuild it in three days, save Yourself, and come down from the cross!" In the same way the chief priests also, along with the scribes, were mocking Him among themselves and saying, "He saved others; He cannot save Himself. Let this Christ, the King of Israel, now come down from the cross, so that we may see and believe!" <u>Those who were crucified with Him were also insulting Him.</u>"

These two men were dying right along with Jesus and they still felt pressured to join the crowd. It is unbelievable to me that some of the last words of two dying men were insults, but it shows how powerful conformity to authority is. Everyone wants to fit in. We learn it in school when we are trained like monkeys to repeat back on tests what the teacher tells us and we don't grow out of it when we get out of school. If anything, the desire to please becomes even stronger because our financial well-being and future is tied to it in an authoritarian society. It is nothing less than terrifying how we have willingly handed over our eternal destinies to people who will throw us to the wolves at the first inkling of any challenge or dissent they perceive coming from us.

Perhaps even worse for Jesus than suffering the abuse of the two criminals beside him was the complete and utter absence of his friends and disciples at his trial and execution. Not one of them showed up to testify on his behalf or support him throughout his torturous ordeal after they had all run off in the Garden of Gethsemane at the time of Jesus' arrest. (Matthew 26:56) They knew him and his teachings better than anyone. If a case was to be made for his innocence on charges of blasphemy, they were the ones to make it. There is strength in numbers. The chief priests could not have accused all of them of blasphemy. That's why they wouldn't arrest Jesus in a public setting. They were afraid of a riot breaking out.

The disciples could have given Jesus the cover he so desperately needed because many of the Jewish people were on Jesus' side. The corrupt chief priests and elders were few in number compared to the masses. If the disciples had shown up in force, they may even have inspired Nicodemus, Joseph of Arimathea or some of the other Pharisee leaders who supported Jesus in secret to come out in the open and speak out against their corrupt colleagues.

It is healthy and good to question authority. We should always be questioning authority because when we do not, it will be misused. Jesus' story is an example of that truth. The Stanford Prison Experiment which was conducted in 1971 and the electric shock experiments of Stanley Milgram conducted in 1963 are both scientific examples of that truth. Both experiments showed how ordinary people will behave in harmful ways toward other human beings when a strong authority figure is directing their actions.

Clearly, the Jewish people did not want Jesus to die. If the institution of the church had given a hearing to all the gospels, this fact would have been made clear and all the anti-Semitic haters over the years that followed would not have been given a safe-haven for their lies and cruelty.

From my own viewpoint, Pilate and the teachers of the law who were at Jesus' fake trial shoulder most of the blame. If we are going to have people with titles ruling over us and claiming they are bound by the rule of law, then their job should be to protect the innocent. Jesus was not convicted on truth. He was condemned with lies and witness tampering. The trial was a farce and the scriptures describing it show the irrationality and mental illness of his accusers.

Rationality, logic and truth will always appear abnormal to irrational, illogical and deceitful people. The thinking process for a gang on the street is no different from that of a gang in power. Both create their own codes of honor to justify their rule over others. Gang membership requires conformity to the irrational code. The only mission and values that inspire the gang are those that protect its members and reinforce its power base. Irrationality of this sort breeds paranoia and fear, both of which warp rationality. In the upside world created by the irrational gang, lies take precedence over truth, reporting misconduct is viewed as snitching, sacrificing one person for the sake of retaining power is considered ethical, feigning friendship to obtain damaging information is considered loyalty, accepting money in return for obedience and silence is smart and taking right action in conflict with the interest of the gang is viewed as mental illness.

It is no accident that psychopathic personalities like Caiaphas and Adolf Hitler use this upside-down dynamic to gaslight their victims into thinking they are at fault for the dysfunction in the relationship. It is insidious and quite mad, but when irrational and illogical liars hold positions of power, they have the final say in who is judged mentally ill.

One man (Caiaphas/Hitler) was able to wield his psychotic influence over intelligent people who had the capability to resist but did not. Once people conform their minds to irrationality and falsehood, then it's game over. That is the point when evil becomes considered good and actions like the holocaust and crucifying innocent men is perceived as right behavior.

9
They Sealed an Empty Tomb

Once Jesus and his disciples were near to Jerusalem for the Passover, in a town called Bethage near the Mount of Olives, Jesus directed two of his disciples to go into the nearby village and get the colt that he told them would be tied up near the entrance to the town. (Matthew 21:1-5, Mark 11:1-10) He told them if they are questioned, to say that the master has need of it and will send it back at once. (Matthew 21:3) When the two are questioned by the owners of the colt in Luke 19:33, they tell the owners what Jesus said and the owners allow them to take it. It is obvious to me from this verse that Jesus arranged with the owners of the colt ahead of time to borrow the colt and Matthew 21:5 tells us why. It was so he could ride into Jerusalem on it to fulfill the prophesy: "Say to Daughter Zion, 'See, your king comes to you, gentle and riding on a donkey, and on a colt, the foal of a donkey.'"

The crowds rushed to greet Jesus crying out, "Hosanna! Blessed is he who comes in the name of the Lord, [even] the king of Israel." Three short days later, the crowds would switch their alliances and cry to have Jesus crucified after "the chief priests and the elders persuaded the crowds to ask for Barabbas but to destroy Jesus." (Matthew 27:20)

This Passover marks Jesus' last Passover in Jerusalem. After his arrest, mock trial and appearance before Pilate, Jesus was placed on the cross at 9:00 a.m. in the morning and pronounced dead at 3:00 p.m. in the afternoon, immediately after drinking from a sponge soaked in vinegar. The Gospel of John describes Jesus' last moments on the cross as follows:

> John 19:28-30: After this, Jesus, knowing that all things had already been accomplished, to fulfill the Scripture, said, "I am thirsty." A jar full of sour wine was standing there; so they put a sponge full of the sour wine upon a branch of hyssop and brought it up to His mouth. Therefore, when Jesus had received the sour wine, He said, "It is finished!" And He bowed His head and gave up His spirit.

Likewise, the gospels of Matthew and Mark both indicate that Jesus died immediately after drinking from a sponge soaked in wine. (Matthew 27:45-50, Mark 15:33-37) The passage in Matthew reads as follows:

> Now from the sixth hour darkness fell upon all the land until the ninth hour. About the ninth hour Jesus cried out with a loud voice, saying, "Eli, Eli, lama sabachthani?" that is, "My God, My God, why have You forsaken Me?" And some of those who were standing there, when they heard it, began saying, "This man is calling for Elijah." Immediately one of them ran, and taking a sponge, he filled it with sour wine and put it on a reed and gave Him a drink. But the rest of them said, "Let us see whether Elijah will come to save Him." And Jesus cried out again with a loud voice and yielded up His spirit.

Similarly, the passage in Mark reads:

> "When the sixth hour came, darkness fell over the whole land until the ninth hour. At the ninth hour Jesus cried

out with a loud voice, "Eloi, Eloi, lama sabachthani?" which is translated, "My God, My God, why have You forsaken Me?" When some of the bystanders heard it, they began saying, "Behold, He is calling for Elijah." Someone ran and filled a sponge with sour wine, put it on a reed, and gave Him a drink, saying, "Let us see whether Elijah will come to take Him down." And Jesus uttered a loud cry and breathed His last."

The first passage from John 19 quoted above is quite illuminating when it says that Jesus asks for a drink once he knows that all parts of the plan for fulfilling the prophesies of Isaiah have been accomplished. Immediately after drinking the wine he says, "It is finished" and breathes his last breath. In each of the passages above, Jesus dies immediately after drinking from a sponge soaked with wine. When Pilate is informed of the death by Joseph of Arimathea who requests the body, Pilate expresses amazement that Jesus has died so quickly, and it causes him to send a centurion to the cross to confirm it. (Mark 15:44-45)

The drinking from the sponge wouldn't mean much on its own but, when you view it in conjunction with the amazement that Pilate expresses that Jesus died so quickly, it makes one wonder what was in the sponge that was given to Jesus to drink. We tend to believe that medicine did not exist until recently. Along with much of the knowledge of the ages, hundreds of years of knowledge in the areas of herbal medicine and natural cures has been abolished in our modern age of reason by labeling it as quackery and new age nonsense by doctors who have advanced through the hierarchies of modern medicine. Although natural cures are often referred to as pseudoscience, the fact of the matter is that the ancient societies of Egypt and Greece had extensive knowledge about the effects of herbal extracts on the human body. Along with using them to cure certain ailments, they were also manipulated for use as both poisons and drugs that altered the state of mind of the persons taking them. In the book, *The Secret Teachings of All Ages*, the author describes how the priesthood used certain drugs that rendered the body of the taker insensible while the person passed through a number of mind-altering experiences before regaining consciousness.[30]

Even though we know very little about Jesus' life, we can surmise that the genius of Jesus was well known by the time he began teaching in the temple at 30 years of age. He was attracting philosophers and doctors as disciples at the age of twelve and John the Baptist said, referring to Jesus, that there is one who will come after him whose sandals he is not worthy to carry. (Matthew 3:11-12) Jesus would have had access to doctors and priests well-versed in the medical sciences, if not he himself. If part of the plan was to ingest a drug mixed into a wine-soaked sponge to mimic death (like the priesthood used to make an initiate's body senseless and lose consciousness) I am sure neither he, Nicodemus or Joseph of Arimathea would have had any problem finding their way to the person who could provide it.

After Jesus is taken down from the cross, Joseph of Arimathea immediately goes to Pilate to ask for the body, which he releases to him. Nicodemus then arrives with one hundred pounds of aloe and myrrh, both of which are healing agents for the skin. Together with Joseph, Mary Magdalene and *another Mary*, they wrap Jesus' body in clean linen and place it in a rock-hewn tomb in which no one has yet been buried. (John 19:39-41, Matthew 27:59-60, Luke 23:53) Joseph then departs after rolling a large stone across the entrance of the tomb, but "Mary Magdalene and the other Mary remain sitting there facing the tomb." (Matthew 27:61)

A bestselling book by a Christian journalist makes the case

that the resurrection is true because it was a woman who discovered the tomb empty. He contends that if the disciples had made the story up, it would have been one of the male disciples who discovered the tomb empty because of the low place women held in society back then. His reasoning is true. He just got the motives wrong.[31]

In the Gnostic Gospel of Mary, Peter tells Mary, "Sister, we know the savior loved you more than any other woman. Tell us the words of the savior that you remember, which you know but we do not, because we have not heard them."[32] In another section, Peter expresses doubt that Jesus would confide in a woman over them, asking the disciples, "Did he really speak with a woman in private, without our knowledge? Should we all turn and listen to her? Did he prefer her to us?" After Mary begins crying because Peter is accusing her of lying about what Jesus told her, Levi steps in and says to Peter, "Peter, you always are angry. Now I see you arguing against this woman like an adversary. If the savior made her worthy, who are you to reject her? Surely the savior knows her well. That is why he has loved her more than us."[33]

These verses indicate that Jesus spoke to Mary in private about matters of which the other disciples were not aware. It also appears from these verses that Mary was loved more than the other disciples. If Jesus loved Mary more than all the other disciples, he probably trusted her more as well. According to Matthew 27:57- 61, we know that Joseph of Arimathea, Mary Magdalene and the other Mary took Jesus' body to the tomb and that Joseph placed the body in the tomb while Mary Magdalene and the other Mary stayed on.

What if Jesus' body was never placed in the tomb? Why would Nicodemus have brought 100 lbs. of healing agents for the skin if the body was dead and to be buried? (John 19:39) Could it be that Jesus was taken off somewhere else to recover and heal while the two Marys were left behind to guard the new tomb that Joseph himself prepared? Was it the job of the two women to make sure no one moved the rock before the allotted time?

When the chief priests went to Pilate and told him that they heard Jesus say that he would rise after three days, Pilate ordered the tomb to be sealed. (Matthew 27:62-66) Is it possible they sealed an empty tomb? According to the account found in Luke 24, Mary Magdalene, Joanna and Mary the mother of James all arrive at the tomb on the first day of the week with spices to embalm the body and they find the tomb empty. The women then go to the disciples to tell them and when Peter and another disciple run to the tomb to see for themselves, they find the burial clothes "and the napkin, that was about his head, not lying with the linen clothes, but wrapped together in a place by itself." (John 20:6-7)

I am not a detective and do not pretend to be one but the scene that Peter walks in on raises all kinds of red flags. Jesus has presumably just risen from the dead in the flesh. He does not know what awaits him outside the tomb, yet he is concerned about being neat and rolling up the cloth before he leaves? It doesn't make sense.

The Gnostic Gospel of James says that Jesus doesn't appear to the disciples until five hundred fifty days later - a full year and a half - while they are all sitting together writing down their recollections.[34] Could Nicodemus and Joseph of Arimathea taken Jesus off somewhere to heal while Mary was left behind to serve as a witness to his resurrection three days later as he had promised?

It is clear that the man who appears to the disciples after the crucifixion is Jesus. He has the scars to prove it to Thomas who cannot believe that Jesus has actually risen from the dead. (John 20:24-29) However, it wasn't just Thomas who doubted. All the disciples expressed doubt that it was really him. (Matthew 28:16-17)

People do not come back from the dead in the flesh. Traditionally, there have been a couple of ways to interpret the resurrection of Jesus. One could either believe that it was God's plan to raise Jesus from the dead in the flesh (although there is nowhere in the Bible where it says that the Messiah would literally come back from the dead) or one could interpret it metaphysically and view it as the spirit of Jesus overcoming death. I think Jesus' own words and behavior after the resurrection prove that he was there in the flesh and since I fall into the camp of people who believe it is impossible for anyone to come back from the dead, I do not believe Jesus ever died. I think he did what he thought he needed to do to physically survive and reinforce his teachings.

For a long time, I was ambivalent about what I believe Jesus did and the choices he made. For one thing, I was raised in the Christian church and had it drilled into me that Jesus was God in human form. God does not act in deceitful ways. Secondly, I had come to love Jesus because it was his teachings that helped my mind to heal from PTSD symptoms I myself suffered from after a traumatic experience in my own life. I didn't want to believe that Jesus, the man, was capable of such deception. Like many people who are so quick to say they would never confess to a crime they didn't commit, I was judging Jesus based on my own experiences and perceptions. I never considered the severe negative stress and intimidation he was subjected to throughout his entire teaching ministry by the Pharisees who wanted to protect their positions of power. Most people do not freely confess to crimes they did not commit. They do it after they have undergone the severe negative stress and fear created in an interrogation room with the interrogators who have rigged the information to achieve a desired result. The person interrogated is not given the same level of information and truth. They assume the police are followers of the law and having police lie about evidence is not a part of their world view, even though lying about evidence has become an acceptable practice by many police departments as a means of obtaining confessions. This is a little-known fact by the general public, many of whom do not believe that an authority figure like a law enforcement officer would ever lie. Since naïve suspects who believe it is outside the realm of possibility that people charged with enforcing the law would lie, they begin to doubt themselves and their own memory.

After researching bullying and mobbing and the effects these behaviors have on the minds of the people who are targeted, I fully understand why Jesus did what I believe he did and why innocent suspects admit to crimes they did not commit. I am tired of putting the burden on victims to get over their experiences and move on. I now save my judgment and wrath for the people who give up the tool of honest communication and truth to resolve conflict, in favor of using the expedient and easy path of targeting and victimizing their fellow human beings in such a cruel manner so that they can protect their own egos and self-interests.

Jesus made the Pharisees see he was not one to be toyed with. He would not be the mouse in their snarling teeth as they played with him like a rag doll. He told them he was the powerful consciousness of the universe, and he refused to take that truth lightly by participating in a rigged game created by human beings with the consciousness of beasts:

> John 8:58-59: "Jesus said to them, "Truly, truly, I say to you, before Abraham was born, I am." Therefore, they picked up stones to throw at Him, but Jesus hid Himself and went out of the temple."

Jesus suffered unspeakable harm at the hands of power

abusers protecting their own selfish interests. They are the very same people who run many workplaces that label fired whistleblowers as disgruntled employees. They run governments that deny the rights of their citizens. They head up academic institutions who punish academicians who part from the party line. They infiltrate religious organizations to preach a theology of hate and inequality. They take over neighborhoods and make the residents live in fear. They put up a blue wall in police departments and refuse to root out corruption. They rape women because they can. They rob the local food mart because they feel entitled. They lie to clients at the behest of their bosses. They cheat on their taxes because they think they should not have to pay. They cheat on their spouses because they are unhappy about the vow they took. They refuse to help someone who is begging them for help and they refuse to forgive when asked for forgiveness. The commonality they all share is that they did not honor the power they individually possessed in each situation to treat others as they themselves would like to be treated if on the receiving end of the power inequality.

Jesus may not have considered the unintended consequences of the strategy he employed to save both himself and his teachings. In fact, I am certain he never anticipated what would eventually happen to his teachings and it should serve as a lesson to us all that actions not grounded in truth will always result in consequences we did not intend and will only serve to detour our individual and collective destiny.

Christianity has completely disregarded the psychological and physical threat Jesus was subjected to daily; knowing the Pharisees were hanging out around him just waiting for him to slip so they could arrest and destroy him. Like the innocent suspect in an interrogation room who is made to feel that the walls are closing in around him and he will suffer the consequences of a guilty person if he does not confess, Jesus was in a pressure cooker that was about to blow its lid when he came up with his fateful strategy. Unfortunately for him and for humanity, his strategy involved deception. Like the innocent person who has relieved the pressure of the interrogation room with a false confession only to find himself faced with the years-long pressure of prison, Jesus solved the immediate problem, but in the process, lost his legacy to men who used the false narrative to build the foundation for a new religion.

All targets of bullying and mobbing tell of the intense anger they feel at the unfairness of the abuse they are receiving. It is anger that builds and builds with nowhere for it to go because the perpetrators of the bullying and mobbing do not allow for any kind of resolution. They feed their own energy with the inner turmoil they create in the minds of their targets. We fail to see that these kinds of people – the beasts of Revelation – enjoy the process of seeking, targeting, abusing and destroying their human prey. A positive resolution would destroy the satisfaction they receive in creating a state of mind in their target(s) that is confused, unfocused, depressed, sad and alienated from everyone else who does not understand the dynamic of what is happening to a human soul undergoing total annihilation. It gives them the satisfaction of knowing they are getting their pound of flesh.

I believe the emotional outbursts that Prof. Westhues says are stereotypical in mobbing cases and are used to turn the tables on the targeted individual are the target's own attempts to relieve the pressure cooker of emotions that have welled up inside their heads. In far too many cases where the target has had access to a weapon, it has resulted in a permanent resolution that is tragic to everyone involved, including the bullied, the bully and their extended family members, colleagues and friends.

I firmly believe Jesus was undergoing all the emotions of a targeted individual and more during his final Passover in Jerusalem, as evidenced by his outburst in the temple and the extreme turmoil he was feeling the Garden of Gethsemane. He didn't have a weapon and he prevented Peter from using his weapon when the soldiers came to arrest him. What he did have was a plan that was put together by a mind that was unfocused, angry and feeling hopeless and helpless, as evidenced by his silence when Pilate questioned him. (Matthew 27:11-14 and Mark 15:1-5)

I believe Jesus was a person trying to survive the system with a very strong spirit of God. His manipulation of his disciples by focusing their minds on the supernatural idea of resurrection so that they would come to see his own resurrection as a sign from God that he was truly the Messiah was a survival technique. However, the thing about deceit is that it is a strategy of ego and the more powerful ego in the equation will always win in the battle of lies.

Peter knew Jesus survived the cross. Caiaphas knew Jesus was alive. Even Saul/Paul probably knew the truth. As I detail in my book, *Patterns of Peter and Paul*, they all used the lie for promoting their own self-interests. Jesus' teachings, legacy, reputation and life were hijacked by the people left behind and there was absolutely nothing he could do to prevent it at that point. He gave it all away when he gave up truth. There was no putting the genie back in the bottle once the church decided to fill the New Testament of the Bible with the letters of Paul whose doctrine focuses solely on the false superhuman aspect of Jesus – an aspect that never existed in truth and reality.

Although I believe Jesus' motive for doing what he did was to preserve his teachings, it was an impossibility because the truth can never be preserved with a lie. Ironically, he knew he was the Messiah, the Pharisees knew he was the Messiah and many Jews believed him to be the Messiah. He didn't need any supernatural sign to prove it. The facts bore witness to it. As Pilate found out, the Jews had all the answers with their Hebrew numbers. The following excerpt is from *The Gospel of Nicodemus, Formerly Called the Acts of Pontius Pilate,* Chapter XXII, that describes a scene that took place between the chief priests and Pilate after Pilate goes to them demanding the truth. It is a rather lengthy, albeit extremely important excerpt in that it proves that the temple leadership knew that Jesus was the Messiah they were all looking for and they hid that fact from humanity because it would be the death knell for them:

"1 Pilate goes to the temple; calls together the rulers, and scribes, and doctors. 2 Commands the gates to be shut; orders the book of the Scriptures; and causes the Jews to relate what they really knew concerning Christ. 14 <u>They declare that they crucified Christ in ignorance, and that they now know him to be the Son of God, according to the testimony of the Scriptures; which, after they put him to death, were examined. AFTER these things Pilate went to the temple of the Jews, and called together all the rulers and scribes, and doctors of the law, and went with them into a chapel of the temple.</u> 2 And commanding that all the gates should be shut, said to them, I have heard that ye have a certain large book in this temple; I desire you, therefore, that it may be brought before me. 3 And when the great book, carried by four ministers of the temple, and adorned with gold and precious stones, was brought, Pilate said to them all, I adjure you by the God of your Fathers, who made and commanded this temple to be built, that ye conceal not the truth from me. 4 Ye know all the things which are written in that book; tell me therefore now, if ye in the Scriptures have found anything of that Jesus whom ye crucified, and at what time of the world he, ought to have come: show it me. 5 Then having sworn Annas and Caiaphas, they commanded all the rest who were with them to go out of the chapel. 6 And they shut the gates of the temple and of the chapel, and said to Pilate, Thou hast made us to swear, O judge, by the building of this temple, to declare to thee that which is true and right. 7 After we had crucified Jesus, not knowing that he was the Son of God, but supposing he wrought his miracles by some magical arts, we summoned a large assembly in this temple. 8 And when we were deliberating among one another about the miracles which Jesus had wrought, we found many witnesses of our own country, who declared that they had seen him alive after his death, and that they heard him discoursing with his disciples, and saw him ascending into the height of the heavens, and entering into them; 9 And we saw two witnesses, whose bodies Jesus raised from the dead, who told us of many strange things which Jesus did among the dead, of which we have a written account in our hands. 10 And it is our custom annually to open this holy book before an assembly, and to search there for the counsel of God. 11 And we found in the first of the seventy books, where Michael the archangel is speaking to the third son of Adam the first man, an account that after five thousand five hundred years, Christ the most beloved son of God was to come on earth, 12 And we further considered, that perhaps he was the very God of Israel who spoke to Moses, Thou shalt make the ark of the testimony; two cubits and a half shall be the length thereof, and a cubit and a half the breadth thereof, and a cubit and a half the height thereof. 13 By these five cubits and a half for the building of the ark of the Old Testament, we perceived and knew that in five thousand years and half (one thousand) years, Jesus Christ was to come in the ark or tabernacle of a body; 14 <u>And so our Scriptures testify that he is the Son of God, and the Lord and King of</u>

Israel. 15 And because after his suffering, our chief priests were surprised at the signs which were wrought by his means, we opened that book to search all the generations down to the generation of Joseph and Mary the mother of Jesus, supposing him to be of the seed of David; 16 And we found the account of the creation, and at what time he made the heaven and the earth, and the first man Adam, and that from thence to the flood, were two thousand seven hundred and forty-eight years. 17 And from the flood to Abraham, nine hundred and twelve. And from Abraham to Moses, four hundred and thirty. And from Moses to David the King, five hundred and ten. 18 And from David to the Babylonish captivity five hundred years. And from the Babylonish captivity to the incarnation of Christ, four hundred years. 19 The sum of all which amounts to five thousand and half (a thousand.) 20 And so it appears, that Jesus whom we crucified, is Jesus Christ the Son of God, and true Almighty God.[35]

The Jews happened upon the secrets of the universe that are kept secret in competitive, egoistic cultures. Jesus decided that it was God's will to share these secrets in the name of reality and truth. Truth. That is what drove Jesus until they drove him to a kind of madness. He was not out for power as some books allege. He was not egoistic at all. He was real to a fault, but the Pharisees made him revert to survival. The passage above says that when the temple priests found out that Jesus was alive and he was the true messiah according to the Hebrew numbers, they realized they had made a terrible mistake in torturing and crucifying him.

Even if their account is true (i.e. that they did not learn Jesus was the Messiah until after they crucified him and not before, which is far more likely) there was no way they could come out and say, "Hey, we made a mistake." Well actually, they could have and that would have resolved everything and put the trajectory back on track. However, their huge egos would not allow them to admit a mistake. It would have put them all at risk, or so their egos told them. In point of fact, it would have been a heroic act that their Jewish followers would have respected. They would have become the leaders the Jewish nation was seeking all along. But no, their egos would never allow it. And thus began the cover-up that has been ongoing ever since.

10
Legacies Destroyed; Reputations Remade

The Jews did have the answers contained in their numbers and scriptures, but their leadership had final say in a hierarchically organized societal structure. If leaders feel threatened by the sharing of information, then they will do all they can to keep it to themselves. In competitive environments, it is not in an organization's best interests to share knowledge and be transparent. Jesus and other truth tellers and whistle blowers are sacrificed for telling the truth. Like the temple priests who served Caiaphas within the temple pyramid, people trying to survive in competitive environments follow the gatekeepers kept at each row of the hierarchical pyramid for fear that going against the leader will serve them up the same fate. They follow the leader instead of the God of Truth, as portrayed in the Garden of Eden allegory, out of fear. If that means falling into the same crippling illusion of lies, abuse and self-preservation the Pharisees fell into in order to survive (either financially, physically, mentally, emotionally or all four) then they do it.

In the words of Jesus, no one can serve two masters. You will either hate the one and love the other or be devoted to one and despise the other. You cannot serve God and mammon. (Matthew 6:24) Mammon, in the context the Bible uses it, encompasses much more than just money. Charles Filmore defines it as, 'The material or worldly thought and belief regarding riches, possessions, and wealth, compared with the true inner riches of the mind, which are the understanding and the realization of the spiritual substance, life and intelligence that lie back of every outer manifestation."[36]

Mammon is neither wealth nor money. It is a state of mind that feeds our desire to survive and thrive in an outer world that has rewired our brains for success in structures that rely on money for their existence. The structures themselves have been created by human beings no greater or worse than ourselves. In that sense, our competitive structures are the foundation of a game that has been set up to create winners and losers. They are not reality. Other human beings just like us, albeit more powerful, have created an illusion we are all taught to navigate within from the time we exit the womb.

That is the significance of Eve's encounter with the serpent in the Garden. Her state of mind changes from one of reality and truth to one of illusion. Eve creates her own illusory structure in the Garden to feed her ego's needs, thoughts and desires once she accepts the serpent's false argument. She then gets Adam to conform to the illusion. In simplistic terms, she rejects serving God to pursue her own self-interests. The caretaker of the Garden makes herself believe she is the Creator of the Garden and thereby has the right to make her own rules (laws) for everyone else in the Garden. One cannot serve God and mammon. You will either hate the one and love the other or be devoted to one and despise the other. God is reality and truth, but 'he' has been turned into a supernatural guy in the sky by ego conscious minds like Eve's who find that reality and truth get in the way when trying to be a winner within the structures.

Jesus told us over 2,000 years ago that the world is upside down because the consciousness of Eve has taken hold within the mind of mankind and made us believe that what is real is unreal and what is unreal is real. Jesus himself said in the Gnostic Gospel of Phillip, dated around the 3rd century and deemed heretical by the Church hierarchy that,

> "The names of worldly things are utterly deceptive, for they turn the heart from what is real to what is unreal. Whoever hears the word god thinks not of what is real but rather of what is unreal. So also with the words father, son, holy spirit, life, light, resurrection, church and all the rest, people do not think of what is real but of what is unreal, [though] the words refer to what is real." [37]

As counter-intuitive as we have been made to believe it is, God is what is real and Jesus's desire to serve God made him the ultimate realist in this man-created, illusory world.

There are a couple of verses in the beginning of the Book of John that are very intriguing to me and seem to indicate that Jesus was a realist for the better part of his life. (John 2:23-25) He was in Jerusalem for the Passover and was beginning to gain a huge following of believers who were amazed at his teachings. It is not surprising that they would be drawn to him. They had become accustomed to being condemned by the knit picky scribes and Pharisees who were quick to point out a law they had broken or a custom they were not following to the letter. All their teachings consisted of 'no, no'. Don't do this. You're not allowed to do that. Now here, in Jesus, was a teacher who was all about the power of saying 'yes, yes' in our lives and not letting worry and anxiety over not having enough stop us from fulfilling our purpose. He taught with the kind of confidence and authority that can only come by way of the truth. Jesus was telling them things like they had the authority to forgive themselves and others. They didn't need someone else to do it for them. (Matthew 9:1-8) They were the source of their own healing through faith in the spirit of truth within. (Matthew 10:18-22) They didn't need to be fearful, anxious or worried about anything if they turn their thinking around and first seek the kingdom of heaven instead of chasing after ego needs that only the human species seems to have hanging over it. (Matthew 6:25-34)

These are amazing teachings, both then and now. The people Jesus spoke to had never before heard anything like them and they hung onto his every word. If Jesus is the son of God in the sense that Christianity portrays him, it is because of his ability to bring us straight to the source of our existence by erasing the fear and anxiety our false consciousness creates in our minds. He opens the flood gates of ideas and possibilities inherent in a life force that is constantly moving, creating and shaping energy to create the optimum physical environment for its consciousness. His teachings give us back our hope and dreams and unlock the talents we were never able to discover when we were locked into the false pyramid climb for our ego's success. By tweaking our perspective, he gives us the reason for why we are here on this earth at this moment in time and provides us with the game plan we should have had all along. Jesus provides us with the means for complete and utter freedom despite the structures because his teachings give us back our reason for being and connect us with the source of our existence so that we can always create a positive momentum for the growth and improvement of ourselves and the people with whom we come into contact.

Where the crowds of downtrodden and hopeless people began to see possibilities, the Pharisees who hounded Jesus only saw Pandora's box opening and they had to shut it before they lost their positions promoting the pyramid scheme which secured their power at the top of the pyramid along with that of their sons and their son's sons. Jesus was and still is the biggest threat to ever come along to those with vested interests in keeping things just the way they are.

It took me a long time to get over my ambivalence about the choices I believe Jesus made. Ultimately though, I have concluded that I cannot blame Jesus for doing what he did. He chose to save his life. He didn't know he would sacrifice the lives of other innocent people like Lazarus in the process.

I do not believe Jesus ever fully realized the depth of the depravity contained within the men who always paraded around as the good men of the temple. I don't think he would have goaded them if he had known their all-consuming desire to please the psychopath they answered to in order to retain their tassels. He would have changed his strategy. Maybe he would have taken some time to get away and think. He could have used those 500+ days to strategize instead of recovering from injuries obtained in an ill-thought-out plan.

Jesus was literally one man against the world. No one man is ever prepared for that kind of battle and they all get destroyed in the end. One must go into battle with knowledge of that truth. There is no running away. There is no winning. There is just the slight possibility that the positive energy of reality and truth one creates in one's lifetime will live on and touch humanity in the way God intended. Evil destroys all that is good under the guise of goodness. It is the way it has always been and always will be on this physical plane. Go within. Live within. Live in the realm of God. It is possible. It is in fact the only way to live as Jesus told Nicodemus. However, if you decide to use survival strategies to protect your own self-interests when they conflict with the self-interests of someone else, then you must always remain aware of the power imbalances that exist and carefully analyze where you yourself fall on the curve.

Jesus was in a fairly good place given the alliances he had cultivated in Joseph of Arimathea, Nicodemus and all the other educated and well-placed doctors and philosophers he gained as disciples over the years. If survival is what one is after, then it worked for him. He survived with his life intact. However, when it comes to protecting personal legacies, that is God's territory. Reputation is in the realm of the human ego's need for survival in this networked world. Legacies are within the realm of God. Giving up truth destroys legacies, both here and in what comes after. You may protect your reputation with deception, but it will always be illusory because this realm is illusory. Reputations are illusory. They protect your survival in this world but if prosperity, growth, renewal, love, righteousness, integrity and eternal well-being are what you are seeking, then you must be willing to forego reputation if that is what is required to retain truth. Being true to yourself and others will protect your legacy. It is in fact the only thing that will protect your legacy. Not a job. Not children. Not some great invention. Not books. Truth and truth alone will protect your mind and soul, no matter the personal price that must be paid for it.

11

Paul Tightened the Noose on Obliterating Jesus' Teachings, but Jesus Gave Him the Rope

Very little is known about the historical Jesus, and it is causing more and more people to think he never existed. However, when viewed through the lens of a bullying problem that has turned into a mobbing, it makes perfect sense that so little is known about him. The good reputations and histories of targets are often wiped out and rewritten by the head of the mob, who then has all his minions in the hierarchy repeat the new storyline. History is always written by the victors which is why the person who said everything we have ever been told is a lie may be right.

The discovery of ancient scrolls like the Nag Hamadi are now giving us a more complete picture of Jesus. In the gospels that made it into the official Christian Bible, we get the impression that Jesus came to see his disciples several days after 'rising from the dead.' However, in the Secret Book of James contained in the Nag Hamadi collection, it says that Jesus did not return to see the disciples until 550 days later while they are all sitting together writing down their recollections:

"The twelve disciples were all sitting together, recalling what the savior had said to each of them, whether in a hidden or an open manner, and organizing it in books. I was writing what is in [my book]. Look, the savior appeared, after he had left [us, while we] were watching for him. Five hundred fifty days after he rose from the dead, we said to him, "Did you depart and leave us?"[38]

The Bible's New Testament only gives us a sampling of these recollections and writings and it is a sampling that was specifically chosen by bishops to further an agenda of growing a religion.[39] They are the ones who chose to include the letters of Paul – a man I firmly believe is the one referred to in Revelation as an impostor apostle. (Revelation 2:2) Paul was not one of the twelve disciples sitting together at a table documenting their recollections when Jesus came to see them 550 days later. But far more importantly, Paul was the one preaching a free message of grace that Jesus specifically disavowed in this meeting. He admonished his disciples for believing that forgiveness and grace can ever come from an outside source by telling them:

"This is also how you can acquire heaven's kingdom for yourselves. Unless you acquire it through knowledge, you will not be able to find it." "Shame on you who are in need of an advocate. Shame on you who stand in need of grace. Blessings will be on those who have spoken out and acquired grace for themselves."[40]

Paul was not a chosen apostle. He was a self-named apostle preaching a message of resurrection and grace that would appeal to a non-Jewish, gentile audience totally ignorant of the teachings of Jesus. I write in detail in my book, *Patterns of Peter and Paul*, about how Paul came into existence and the important role he played in proselytizing to a wide-open and captive gentile audience who had no previous knowledge or assumptions. They were a blank slate upon which Paul could implant any information he liked without blow-back about such things as facts. A thorough reading of Paul's own letters, which comprise most of the books of the New Testament outside the Gospels of Matthew, Mark, Luke and John; will show just how thoroughly he disregards facts when citing scriptures to back up his claims. None of the scriptures he cites are cited verbatim and they are all manipulated to serve his agenda as a church builder for the non-Jewish gentiles.

Paul may have tightened the noose on the obliteration of Jesus' teachings and legacy, but Jesus himself may have given him the rope by providing him with the narrative, false as it was. When Jesus appears to the disciples while they are writing what they remember, he says to them:

> "Now He said to them, "These are My words which I spoke to you while I was still with you, that all things which are written about Me in the Law of Moses and the Prophets and the Psalms must be fulfilled." Then He opened their minds to understand the Scriptures, and He said to them, "Thus it is written, that the Christ would suffer and rise again from the dead on the third day, and that repentance for forgiveness of sins would be proclaimed in His name to all the nations, beginning from Jerusalem You are witnesses of these things." (Luke 24:44-48)

It has taken me a long time to accept, but it was Jesus who opened their minds to understand the changed message. Jesus created the confusion that has given rise to the numerous sects of Christianity. Jesus also created Paul who had to come up with fanciful and misquoted scriptures to back-up a story told by Jesus that does not appear anywhere in the Scriptures. Nowhere in the Bible does it say the Messiah will suffer and rise from the dead on the third day outside of Jesus planting this idea in the heads of his disciples by manipulating the story of Jonah found in the Old Testament Book of Jonah. Jesus didn't open their minds to understanding the scriptures as he claims in the above passage from Luke. He closed their minds to the truth he had taught them and changed their minds to accepting a lie. He manipulated the story of Jonah to create the supernatural sign that he was the much-awaited Messiah. He fell back on his Pharisaic training which was steeped in the belief of supernatural signs like resurrections, angels and spirits. (Acts 23:7-8) He undid every truth about the reality of God that he dedicated his life to teaching. He ended up doing what he so strongly and courageously fought against in all his verbal battles with the Pharisees. He reinforced the idea of the supernatural guy in the sky that Pharisees embraced. His ego's survival instincts destroyed the truth he fought so hard to tell.

Caiaphas had his false witnesses and Jesus now had his. The genie was out of the bottle as soon as Jesus spoke those words and no amount of trying to take them back, as he does in his testimony to John in Revelation, could ever get the genie back in the bottle. The message of free grace and forgiveness spread like wildfire in a world where our own egos have us doing such harmful things to ourselves and fellow human beings in the name of survival, self-interest and winning at all costs.

Like all mobbing victims who lose everything at the hands of powerful forces whose goal it is to make them lose everything (reputation included) Jesus was a changed man after the crucifixion. The man who showed up to his disciples as they are writing what they remember of their teacher is a decidedly different man from the one who helped Nicodemus take the scales from his eyes and the one who spoke to the Samaritan woman by the well, as found in John, Chapter 4. In that story, Jesus is speaking with a woman by a well when his disciples arrive. When his disciples urge him to eat, he tells them, "I have food to eat of which you do not know....My food is to do the will of the one who sent me and to finish his work."

Now, contrast that response to what he says to his disciples when he returns to them 550 days after the crucifixion, while they are all sitting around a table writing down their recollections. Some people who have studied the Bible have noted how unextraordinary such an extraordinary event as Jesus' appearance to his disciples after the crucifixion comes across in the New Testament. Below is a passage from Luke 24:36-43 that portrays the blandness of this 'extraordinary' event:

> "While they were telling these things, He Himself stood in their midst and said to them, "Peace be to you." But they were startled and frightened and thought that they were seeing a spirit. And He said to them, "Why are you troubled, and why do doubts arise in your hearts? See My hands and My feet, that it is I Myself; touch Me and see, for a spirit does not have flesh and bones as you see that I have." And when He had said this, He showed them His hands and His feet. While they still could not believe it because of their joy and amazement, He said to them, "Have you anything here to eat?" They gave Him a piece of a broiled fish; and He took it and ate it before them."

Got anything to eat? That sentence spoken by Jesus practically broke my heart when I read it. Got anything to eat? That is all that is left to say from a man whose spirit was broken on the cross. That was all that was left to be said by a man who was spit on, whipped, ridiculed, lied to and marked for execution by colleagues who he grew up with, studied with, worked and lived with. That was all he had to ask of the twelve men who abandoned him in his darkest hours and were now hiding out for fear of what their association with him might cost them. Got anything to eat? The all-important words of survival in this physical world where betrayal can leave you destitute – mind, body and soul. Perhaps they are the words of a person who learns the truth about an automaton-like, follow-the-leader kind of human nature he never thought could possibly exist. They are quite possibly the words of a person who learns the truth of his own human nature.

According to Mark 16:9-14, the only reason he appeared before the disciples after the crucifixion was to admonish them for not believing the witnesses to his resurrection:

> "Now after He had risen early on the first day of the week, He first appeared to Mary Magdalene, from whom He had cast out seven demons. She went and reported to those who had been with Him, while they were mourning and weeping. When they heard that He was alive and had been seen by her, they refused to believe it. After that, He appeared in a different form to two of them while they were walking along on their way to the country. They went away and reported it to the others, but they did not believe them either. Afterward He appeared to the eleven themselves as they were reclining at the table; and He reproached them for their unbelief and hardness of heart, because they had not believed those who had seen Him after He had risen."

When I read this passage in Mark, I am left with the feeling that Jesus would never have shown up in the flesh if his disciples had believed the testimony of Mary Magdalene and the two men who claimed to have talked to him on the Road to Emmaus a day or so after his grave was discovered empty. (Luke 24:13-35) Just like with Lazarus, Jesus wanted the testimony of witnesses to be enough but when the disciples didn't believe the witness testimony, then he had to take matters into his own hands and show up *in the flesh* so they could witness him for themselves. Even so, some of them still didn't believe and continue not to believe to this day. It is in fact what drove me and others of my generation away from the church. How am I expected to believe that one man saved the world by rising from the dead and all I have to do is declare that I believe in the story to gain entry into heaven? It is a ludicrous proposition when perceived through the eyes of reason. Human beings do not rise from the dead and even if they do, given the accounts of many near-death experiencers, that fact alone does not make one the savior of all mankind.

Jesus violated his basic tenet. He took matters into his own hands when they were best left up to the spirit of reality and truth. His disciples were writing their recollections. Jesus had succeeded in teaching them and they were dedicating themselves to teaching others by memorializing his teachings. The waters became all muddied with Jesus' attempt to manipulate their understanding with the supernatural sign he used to placate the Pharisees' need for a sign. Waters always become muddied when we manipulate the truth. No one knows what to believe and it allows them to believe their own versions of the truth. That is what world views and religions are – some version of the truth (translate: perception). When truth becomes perception, it becomes very easy for people at the top of the hierarchy to change it to a version that best fits their individual agendas.

This man who appears before the disciples to "upbraid them

with their unbelief and hardness of heart" bears no resemblance to the Jesus who came out of the wilderness with the desire to dedicate his life to teaching the truth about God, but it does resemble someone who has had his life upended by corrupt and powerful individuals who were out to destroy him, and anyone who helped him, simply because he was spreading the truth they wanted so desperately to keep hidden in the holy books they locked away and took out but once a year.

We know Lazarus was killed and in the Gospel of Nicodemus contained in the Nag Hammadi collection of gospels, it says that Nicodemus and Joseph of Arimathea were both jailed because they came to Jesus's aid after the crucifixion.

> CHAPTER IX. 1The Jews angry with Nicodemus; 5 and with, Joseph of Arimathaea, 7 whom they imprison. WHEN the unjust Jews heard that Joseph had begged and buried the body of Jesus, they sought after Nicodemus, and those fifteen men who had testified before the governor, that Jesus was not born through fornication, and other good persons who had shown any good actions towards him. 2 But when they all concealed themselves through fear of the Jews, Nicodemus alone showed himself to them, and said, How can such persons as these enter into the synagogue? 3 The Jews answered him, But how durst thou enter into the synagogue, who wast a confederate with Christ? Let thy lot be along with him in the other world. 4 Nicodemus answered, Amen; so may it be, that I may have my lot with him in his kingdom. 5 In like manner Joseph, when he came to the Jews, said to them, Why are ye angry with me for desiring the body of Jesus of Pilate? Behold, I have put him in my tomb, and wrapped him up in clean linen, and put a stone at the door of the sepulchre: 6 I have acted rightly towards him; but ye have acted unjustly against that just person,

in crucifying him, giving him vinegar to drink, crowning him with thorns, tearing his body with whips, and praying down the guilt of his blood upon you. 7 The Jews at the hearing of this were disquieted and troubled; and they seized Joseph, and commanded him to be put in custody."[41]

The last sentence of the passage above says the Jews (chief priests) were disquieted and troubled upon being reminded of what they did to Jesus. Whenever these monsters are reminded of their unjust cruelty against another human being, they get 'disquieted and troubled' and punish the person(s) reminding them of their sins or force them into silence. That is why killing the messenger then punishing anyone who refuses to accept and spread the false narrative regarding the messenger is a time-honored strategy of bullies because it creates the enablers and bystanders of our world and keeps real change from happening.

Although I have spent an entire book talking about how Jesus was mobbed by the power structure of his day, the strategies used by the Pharisees in the mobbing are not confined to mobbing. They are the same strategies used by any individual or group that wants to protect their personal turf.

We hear a lot these days about how narcissists, psychopaths and sociopaths think and the destruction they cause among their fellow human beings. We love our labels, so we label these power abusers as narcissistic, sociopathic and psychopathic and we call their behaviors spousal abuse, criminal fraud, bullying or whatever. We can label their behaviors anything we want but what we are really talking about is patterns of thought that result in behaviors as old as mankind itself. The Bible is filled with people who display these behaviors but instead of analyzing their thought patterns so that we can protect ourselves and others from them, every power abuser in the world who has attained a position of power has marginalized the book so that its true message remains as hidden as it was when Jesus was alive.

12
If David Calls Him Lord, How Can He Be His Son?

Jesus delighted the crowds wherever he went, and he did it with the simple logic of a man who has done the work of examining world views and then passing them through the prism of reason and facts. In Mark 10:35-37, Jesus is teaching in the temple area and he asks the people who have gathered there a question: How can the scribes claim that the Messiah is the son of David when David himself calls him Lord? Verse 37 says that the great crowd heard this with delight. Truth is always delightful and refreshing, particularly when it is so obvious, yet it has been so manipulatively spun to conform to certain world views and agendas. I think that is the reason why comedians who point out obvious truths with their humor are the funniest of all.

Jesus obviously was not the son of David but that does not change the fact that his story and that of King David are both stories of two exceptional men who were bullied by the powerful elite of their day. The parallels between King David and Jesus are striking, yet they are lost to the fables we all learn in Sunday School. When most of us recall the story of King David, all we remember is the childhood story we heard about how a boy named David killed a giant named Goliath with his slingshot. That was merely one incident in the life of a very complex Bible character who overcomes the evil of someone trying to harm him by acting strategically and never letting himself give into the same evil motives driving his enemy.

King Saul, David's predecessor, was jealous of David and angry at him for what he perceived as his theft of the affections of Samuel, Saul's mentor and friend. Samuel turned on Saul when Saul made a value judgment in the heat of battle after receiving explicit instructions from Samuel before the battle to do otherwise. Instead of taking his anger out on the responsible party, Saul took it out on David, the person who Samuel took as his protege after rejecting Saul. (David's story can be found in the Books of 1 Samuel and 2 Samuel)

After David slayed the giant everyone thought couldn't be slain, he came home to adoring women from all the cities who sang to him: "Saul has slain his thousands. David his tens of thousands." Saul became very angry and resentful after hearing the song. 1 Samuel 18:8-9 says Saul began thinking, "They give David tens of thousands, but only thousands to me. All that remains for him is the kingship. From that day on, Saul kept a jealous eye on David." The next day, Saul failed in one of several attempts he made to kill David out of rage.

David never retaliated against Saul's attempts to kill him. Instead, he got away from the situation by leaving town until it was safe to come back, which was many years later. If David had killed Saul, who was the king, David would have begun a bloodbath that most likely would have ended in his own violent death. Unless a person is willing to go down in complete defeat, it is best to get away from people who are abusing their power because the odds are stacked against you as a person with less power. The game is set up for the power abusers to win. It is not cowardice to walk away from a no-win situation. It is a smart strategy that keeps your own well-being intact. It may not be fair and it may not be just, but it is the way it is in hierarchical-structured environments where all the power lies in the hands of other people. Unless you can rally behind you an army of supporters who will testify on your behalf – a feat Jesus was unable to do with his army of disciples and supporters – then the matter is best left to time and truth.

I could take each and every story in the Bible and analyze it in this way. It is, in fact, the way every Bible story should be analyzed – by the message it is giving and the false assumptions it is questioning. It is destructive to interpret the Bible in a literal, historical sense because it distorts the message into something that is untrue and non-truth is always destructive. Jesus' story is told over and over again daily and we fail to connect the dots.

Many people who are bullied, abused and taken advantage of are naïve. They believe that people are naturally good and would never intentionally set out to harm them for no reason. This view is not only held by the naive; it is a view that is maintained by our society at large. We are constantly told to think positively and things will turn out just fine. That is good as far as it goes but it fails to factor in that there are bad people with bad motives out there and competitive and hierarchically structured organizations are fertile breeding grounds for these types of people. Failing to account for this fact dooms the naive target of a power abuser to months, if not years, of suffering as the bullying continues unabated.

As I learned more about Jesus and the true nature of good and evil, I came to realize that evil is just as real as good and it is incumbent on us to face reality in all its forms. Naivety is a form of escape from reality. Jesus was anything but the saccharin sweet person many people perceive him as being. He was a hardcore realist who embraced conflict because conflict is an inevitability of confronting evil in all its forms in an egocentric culture. Sweet people get trampled. Fearless and courageous people create life on their terms because when they do the cost-benefit analysis, failure to follow truth is not an option.

Everything Jesus teaches us is at the individual soul level. He was not concerned with what others do in a general sense; he was concerned with how each person cares for his own consciousness. So often, when I have heard ministers preach on "turning the other cheek", they have put the emphasis on others' bad behavior and how we should react to that bad behavior. Essentially, they tell us to ignore the behavior and it will go away. This philosophy has been so ingrained in our society to the point that we tell our children when they are being mistreated by others, to "just ignore them and they'll stop." But they don't stop. Power abusers are relentless in their pursuit to destroy your confidence and gain the upper hand through obfuscation, deceit, taunts and other forms of aggression; both subtle and in-your-face because that is what gives them their win. Ignoring them just makes them more determined. My research on the subject has led me to believe that the only way for a person to deal with bullying and mobbing is to know that even as the stormy seas cast you about, you will safely arrive at the other shore if you retain the integrity of their core consciousness. Give the power abusers their win but never at the expense of your own well-being. Have faith that there an infinite number of turns you can take in this life that will all lead you to your destiny if you retain your faith in the source code of your being and follow it in truth. It is when doubt and fear creep into your core that the door is opened to the hopelessness and despair that warp our minds and cause us to think thoughts and take actions that we would not otherwise think and take in moments of rationality, confidence and calm. These kinds of thoughts will always lead us further from the paradise our minds are at home in.

Our minds are where heaven is. It is not up in the sky

somewhere with the guy who is wreaking vengeance on our souls for not following his rules, as the literal interpretation of the Bible has us believing. It is within the consciousness of life that permeates our world and our universe. We destroy that consciousness at our own peril.

Good conquers evil one mind at a time. It has always been that way and always will be that way. David was the king of the Jews because he conquered evil with good within himself. We can physically destroy dictators and other power abusers we perceive as evil but there will always be millions of people to take their place in close-ended pyramids of power that have replaced our source of life with false voices of authority to whom we must submit if we want to survive.

To the extent that anyone seeks to replicate the organizational and behavioral strategies inherent in bullying and mobbing to build an empire of power - whether at the level of one, the level of a family, the level of a nation or the level of the world - we will continue to see the consciousness of survival played out and people like Leif and Jesus getting persecuted simply for being the people they are. As long as we go after the people we perceive as the evildoers, we will continue to avoid looking at the evil within ourselves. As long as we punish individual behavior rather than doing the arduous and costly exercise of identifying corrupted patterns of thought within ourselves, so that they can be rooted out and destroyed, then we will continue to create upside-down environments that perceive the logical source code of life and growth as bad and the corrupted processes of thought created by our need to survive within corrupted structures as good.

It was his jealous co-worker's success in turning the tables upside down and getting the entire workforce to view Leif as incompetent and crazy that made them successful in forcing Leif from the workplace. They got their win at the price of one man's life. Caiaphas and his minions got their win at the same price. It is the price that all corrupted power brokers are willing to pay to win and retain their locus of control.

The Jewish leaders had the answer all along. It was contained within their ancient scriptures that Jesus was interpreting as they should be interpreted. They wanted to keep that knowledge to them- selves and Jesus was out there spreading it like wildfire. Containment became the name of the game once Caiaphas became involved. Jesus' fate was sealed within the structures of survival. Now is the time for his Christ consciousness to rise out of the ashes of a history that was written for him and a legacy that was stolen from him by others. Now is the time for the life-saving teachings of Jesus to be reclaimed from some early disciples who thought that just a little compromise wouldn't hurt anything. Now is the time to acquire grace for ourselves by acquiring knowledge of the human mind that science is providing to us daily with its discoveries concerning energy, consciousness and the universe. Now is the time for us to hear the truth that our own Pharisaic minds want to deny for fear of what it will cost us in terms of survival in this world. However, first we must hear it within ourselves. Like the concept of being born again that was so hard for Nicodemus to grasp, we must return to the source code of our being so that we can ourselves live in logic, reality and truth. That is the only way an army of supporters within mankind itself will be able to topple and destroy the hierarchies of power that have their networked web of bystanders and enablers doing their bidding at every level of society. That is the time when the Creator will redeem its throne and the Garden of Eden it envisioned when our world was created will finally be realized in the hearts and minds of all the men and women who inhabit it.

The End

Bibliography

1   "Galileo Galilei." Wikipedia, the Free Encyclopedia. N.p., n.d.
    Web. 12 Mar. 2014.
    <http://en.wikipedia.org/wiki/Galileo_galilei>.
2   Easton, M. G. (n.d.). Repentance Definition and Meaning -
    Bible Dictionary. Retrieved October 11, 2017, from
    http://www.bibles- tudytools.com/dictionary/repentance.
3   Scutt, J. (2004, October). Mediocrity and the 'no change'
    Principle: a Recipe for Mobbing. Workplace Mobbing Australia
    Conference, 2004. Retrieved October 11, 2017, from
    http://www.workplacemobbing.com.
4   Carruthers, Bob (2011-11-13). The Nuremberg Trials - The
    Complete Proceedings Vol 4: Individual Responsibility of the
    Defendants (The Third Reich from Original Sources) (Kindle
    Locations 5323-5337). Coda Books Ltd. Kindle Edition.
5   Davenport, N., Schwartz, R. D., Elliott, G. P., Leymann, H., &
    Vidali, S. (2005). Mobbing: emotional abuse in the American
    workplace. Ames, IA: Civil Society Publishing.
6   Leymann, H. (2009, February 13). Mobbing and Psychological
    Terror at Workplaces. Retrieved October 11, 2017, from
    http://www.mobbingportal.com/leymannmain.html.
7   Ibid.
8   Westhues, K. (n.d.). At the Mercy of the Mob. Retrieved
    October 11, 2017, from http://kwesthues.com/ohs-canada.
9   Namie, G., & Namie, R. (2009). The bully at work: what you
    can do to stop the hurt and reclaim your dignity on the job.
    Naperville, IL: Sourcebooks.
10 Shallcross, L., Ramsay, S., & Barker, M. (2010, January 01). A
    Proactive Response to the Mobbing Problem: A Guide for HR
    Managers. Retrieved October 11, 2017, from
    https://www.researchgate.net/
11 Westhues, K. (n.d.). At the Mercy of the Mob. Retrieved
    October 11, 2017, from http://kwesthues.com/ohs-canada.
12 Ibid.

13 Reed, A. (2015, July 05). AMA issues new threat to outspoken holistic doctors. Retrieved October 27, 2017, from https://www.naturalhealth365.com

14 Wake, William (2012-05-17). Forbidden books of the original New Testament (p. 115). Kindle Edition.

15 Joseph, P. (Director). (2007). Zeitgeist: The Movie [Motion picture]. Screenwriter: Peter Joseph.

16 Ibid.

17 John 19:38. [Also see The Gospel Of Nicodemus, Formerly Called The Acts Of Pontius Pilate. Wake, William (2012-05-17). Forbidden books of the original New Testament for additional scriptures that make mention of both men and what happened to them after the crucifixion of Jesus.]

18 Leymann, H. (2009, February 13). Mobbing and Psychological Terror at Workplaces. Retrieved October 11, 2017, from http://www.mobbingportal.com/leymannmain.html.

19 Kershaw, Alex (2010-10-26). The Envoy: The Epic Rescue of the Last Jews of Europe in the Desperate Closing Months of World War II (p. 223). Perseus Books Group. Kindle Edition.

20 Yorum, Barak, M.D and Szor, Henry, M.D., Lifelong posttraumatic stress disorder: evidence from aging Holocaust survivors, Published on the web, March 2000, Lifelong posttraumatic stress disorder: evidence from aging Holocaust survivors - PMC (nih.gov)

21 (n.d.). Retrieved October 12, 2017, from http://www.bullyonline.org/stress/ptsd.htm 24

22 Ibid.

23 Westhues, Prof. Kenneth. At the Mercy of the Mob: A Summary of Research on Workplace Mobbing. Published in OHS Canada, Canada's Occupational Health & Safety Magazine, Vol. 18, No. 8, December 2002, pp. 30-36. Published on the web, January 2003, http://www.overcomebullying.org/mobbing-bullying-research.html

24 (n.d.). Retrieved October 12, 2017, https://en.wikipedia.org/wiki/Irving_Janis.

25 http://hillconsultinggroup.org/assets/pdfs/articles/8-symptoms- group-think.pdf. Eight Main Symptoms of Group Think, Janis, I. L. & Mann, L. (1977). Decision making: A psychological analysis of conflict, choice, and commitment. New York: Free Press.

26 Wake, William (2012-05-17). Forbidden books of the original New Testament (pp. 103-104). Kindle Edition.

27 Ibid.

28 Carruthers, Bob (2011-11-13). The Nuremberg Trials - The Complete Proceedings Vol 4: Individual Responsibility of the Defendants (The Third Reich from Original Sources) (Kindle Locations 1492-1497). Coda Books Ltd. Kindle Edition.

29 Ibid.

30 Hall, M. P. (2011). The Secret Teachings of all Ages: an encyclopedic outline of Masonic, Hermetic, Qabbalistic and Rosicrucian symbolical philosophy: being an interpretation of the secret teachings concealed within the rituals, allegories, and mysteries of the ages. Place of publication not identified: Pacific Pub. Studio.

31 Strobel, Lee. (2016). The Case for Christ: A Journalist's Personal Investigation of the Evidence for Jesus, Zondervan.

32 Meyer, Marvin. The Gnostic Gospels of Jesus. Gospel of Mary. Kindle. Location 875 of 5611, p. 38 of 344.

33 Meyer, Marvin. The Gnostic Gospels of Jesus. Gospel of Mary. Location 914 of 5611, p. 42 of 344.

34 Meyer, Marvin. The Gnostic Gospels of Jesus. Gospel of James. Kindle. Location 2879 of 5611.

35 Wake, William (2012-05-17). Forbidden books of the original New Testament (pp. 2-4). Kindle Edition.

36 Filmore, Charles. The Revealing Word. A Dictionary of Metaphysical Terms (Sacred Books). Kindle. Loc. 4744.

37 Wake, William (2012-05-17). Forbidden books of the original New Testament (pp. 115-116). Kindle Edition.

38 Meyer, Marvin. The Gnostic Gospels of Jesus. Gospel of James. Kindle. Location 2889 of 5611, p. 192 of 344.

39 Wake, William (2012-05-17). Forbidden books of the original
    New Testament (pp. 1-3). Kindle Edition.
40 Meyer, Marvin. The Gnostic Gospels of Jesus. Gospel of
    James. Kindle. Location 2979 of 5611, p. 198 of 344.
41 Wake, William (2012-05-17). Forbidden books of the original
    New Testament (pp. 115-116). Kindle Edition.

www.ingramcontent.com/pod-product-compliance
Lightning Source LLC
Chambersburg PA
CBHW060256050426
42448CB00009B/1660

9780692971956